KEY
WOMEN
WRITERS
EDITOR: SUE ROE

COLETTE

NICOLE WARD JOUVE

Reader in English Literature
University of York

Indiana University Press
Bloomington and Indianapolis

Manufactured in Great Britian

Library of Congress Cataloging-in-Publication Data

Ward Jouve, Nicole.
  Colette.

  1. Colette, 1873–1954—Criticism and interpretation.
2. Women and literature—France. I. Title.
PQ2605.028Z92 1987   848′.91209   **86-46240**
ISBN 0-253-30102-5
ISBN 0-253-25452-3 (pbk.)

1 2 3 4 5   91 90 89 88 87

For my mother and my father,
with love

Titles in the Key Women Writers Series

Key Women Writers

Series Editor: Sue Roe

The *Key Women Writers* series has developed in a spirit of challenge, exploration and interrogation. Looking again at the work of women writers with established places in the mainstream of the literary tradition, the series asks, in what ways can such writers be regarded as feminist? Does their status as canonical writers ignore the notion that there are ways of writing and thinking which are specific to women? Or is it the case that such writers have integrated within their writing a feminist perspective which so subtly maintains its place that these are writers who have, hitherto, been largely misread?

In answering these questions, each volume in the series is attentive to aspects of composition such as style and voice, as well as to the ideas and issues to emerge out of women's writing practice. For while recent developments in literary and feminist theory have played a significant part in the creation of the series, feminist theory represents no specific methodology, but rather an opportunity to broaden our range of responses to the issues of history, psychology and gender which have always engaged women writers. A new and creative dynamics between a woman critic and her female subject has been made possible by recent developments in feminist theory, and the series seeks to reflect the

vii

important critical insights which have emerged out of this new, essentially feminist, style of engagement.

It is not always the case that literary theory can be directly transposed from its sources in other disciplines to the practice of reading writing by women. The series investigates the possibility that a distinction may need to be made between feminist politics and the literary criticism of women's writing which has not, up to now, been sufficiently emphasized. Feminist reading, as well as feminist writing, still needs to be constantly interpreted and re-interpreted. The complexity and range of choices implicit in this procedure are represented throughout the series. As works of criticism, all the volumes in the series represent wide-ranging and creative styles of discourse, seeking at all times to express the particular resonances and perspectives of individual women writers.

Sue Roe

Contents

ix

Acknowledgements

I wish to thank my mother, who got me books by Colette, on Colette, articles, newspaper cuttings: hunting through bookshops in Marseilles and Paris, producing a lifeline of material and caring for me. And my father, who got caught at the game. I owe him books on Willy, the abbé Mugnier or Raymond Oliver's memoirs, mixed with his own travel or gastronomical memories.

All critical books carry a subtext: you find it in the gaps between the text and the bibliography. How did s/he use such a book? what did s/he make of such an article? you think, leafing through pages of bibliography, wondering how those texts were read, why this, and not that, is acknowledged? Bees 'pillotent' flowers, wrote Montaigne, then they make the honey, which is all theirs: it is no longer thyme, nor marjoram. Like Montaigne writing his *Essays* and, I imagine, like most critics, I began writing in the margins of Colette. I conducted silent but impassioned dialogues with those who had written about her, I formulated ideas, had them dawn upon me, as I was talking with friends, colleagues, students. Then the dialogues quietened down and my margins grew into the main text and the Colette became quotations. There have been many more sources of thyme and marjoram than shows in the bibliography, and I couldn't begin to acknowledge all the life exchanges that have led to this book. To all who gave to me, who fed me, I gratefully give thanks.

Grateful acknowledgement is made to Albin Michel for permission to translate directly from the following: *Claudine à l'école, La Vagabonde* and *Claudine in Paris*, reference being made to the Pléiade collected works of Colette, vol. I, © Albin Michel for these works; to Hachette for permission to translate from the same edition of *Les Vrilles de la vigne*, copyright © Hachette, 1961 and from their 1979 edition of *Le Pur et l'impur*, © Hachette, 1979; to Mercure de France for permission to translate from *Claudine en ménage* and *La Retraite sentimentale*, © Mercure de France (quotations also from the Pléiade edition); and to Fayard for permission to quote and translate from *Bella-Vista* and *Le Journal à rebours*, vol. XII of *Oeuvres complètes* and from *Le Fanal bleu*, vol. XIV of the same edition, Flammarion 1950, © Fayard.

Permission is gratefully acknowledged for permission to quote from the following: *Duo and The Toutonier*, translated by Margaret Crosland, © Peter Owen, Ltd, reference being made to the Women's Press edition and © 1975, The Bobbs-Merrill Company, Inc.; *My Apprenticeships*, translated by Helen Beauclerk, © Martin Secker and Warburg Ltd, 1957 (Penguin Books); *My Mother's House*, translated by Una Vincenzo Troubridge and Enid McLeod, and *Sido*, translated by Enid McLeod, © Martin Secker and Warburg Ltd, 1953 (both in a one-volume Penguin); *Break of Day*, translated by Enid McLeod, © Martin Secker and Warburg Ltd, 1961, edition by The Women's Press; *The Ripening Seed*, translated by Roger Senhouse, © Martin Secker and Warburg, Ltd, 1955; *Claudine Married*, translated by Antonia White, © Martin Secker and Warburg Ltd, 1960; *Chéri and The Last of Chéri*, translated by Roger

Acknowledgements

Senhouse © Martin Secker and Warburg Ltd, 1951, Penguin edition; *The Vagabond*, translated by Enid McLeod, © Martin Secker and Warburg Ltd, 1954, Penguin edition; *Chance Acquaintances* and *Julie de Carneilhan*, translated by Patrick Leigh Fermor, © Martin Secker and Warburg Ltd, 1952, Penguin edition; *The Stories of Colette*, translated by Antonia White, © Secker and Warburg Ltd, 1958; *Creatures Great and Small*, translated by Enid McLeod, © Martin Secker and Warburg Ltd, 1951.

Excerpts from the following are also reprinted by permission of Farrar, Straus and Giroux, Inc.: *Break of Day* by Colette, translated by Enid McLeod. English translation copyright © 1961, 1963 by Martin Secker and Warburg Ltd; *Chéri* and *The Last of Chéri* by Colette. English translation copyright 1951 by Farrar, Straus and Young. Copyright renewed © 1982 by Farrar, Straus and Giroux, Inc.; *The Complete Claudine* by Colette. Original English translation copyright © 1976 by Farrar, Straus and Giroux, Inc. Copyright © 1958, 1960, 1962 by Martin, Secker and Warburg Ltd; *Gigi/Julie de Carneilhan/Chance Acquaintances* by Colette, translated by Roger Senhouse. English translation copyright 1952 by Farrar, Straus and Young, Inc. Copyright renewed © 1980 by Farrar, Straus and Giroux, Inc.; *My Apprenticeships* by Colette, translated by Helen Beauclerk. English translation copyright © 1957 by Martin Secker and Warburg Ltd; *Sido* and *My Mother's House* by Colette, translated by Enid McLeod and Una Vincenzo Troubridge. Copyright 1953, renewed © 1981 by Farrar, Straus and Giroux, Inc.; *The Ripening Seed* by Colette, translated by Roger Senhouse. English translation copyright 1955 by Farrar Straus and Cudahy. Copyright renewed © 1983 by Farrar, Straus and Giroux, Inc.; *The Tender Shoot* by Colette, translated by Antonia White. Copyright © 1958 by Martin Secker and Warburg Ltd. Copyright renewed

Acknowledgements

Abbreviations

I have tried to use the most readily available translations of Colette in English, and the standard or most readily available editions in French when I had a particular point to make and needed to translate myself in order to steer closer to the original text. All copyrights are as stated in the list of acknowledgements. Translations are as listed there.

My Appr	: *My Apprenticeships and Music-Hall Sidelights*, Penguin Books
My M's H	: *My Mother's House*, Penguin Books
Sido	: *Sido*, in the same Penguin Books volume as *My Mother's House*
B of D	: *Break of Day*, The Women's Press
RS	: *The Ripening Seed*, Secker and Warburg
C at S	: *Claudine At School*, in the Pléiade *Oeuvres* vol. I, my translation
CM	: *Claudine Married*, Secker and Warburg
Chéri	: *Chéri and The Last of Chéri*, Penguin Books
V	: *The Vagabond*, Penguin Books
P&I	: *Le Pur et l'impur*, Hachette, 1979. My translation
Ch Acq	: *Chance Acquaintances*, Penguin Books
J de C	: *Julie de Carneilhan*, Penguin, same volume as *Chance Acquaintances*

Abbreviations

BV	: *Bella-Vista*, Flammarion, *Oeuvres complètes*, XII, my translation
SC	: *The Stories of Colette*, Secker and Warburg
JR	: *Le Journal à rebours (Looking Backwards*, Flammarion, *Oeuvres complètes*, my translation from vol. XII
FB	: *Le Fanal bleu (The Blue Lantern)* Flammarion, *Oeuvres complètes* XIV my translation
Duo	: *Due and The Toutonier*, The Women's Press
CGS	: *Creatures Great and Small*, Secker and Warburg
PL	: Pléiade Edition of Colette's *Oeuvres* Gallimard, vol. I, 1984 (Copyright as stated in the list of acknowledgements)
L of Ch	: *Last of Chéri*, same volume as *Chéri*, Penguin

Introduction: A Woman Writer

A look at the titles is enough. *Minne. Mitsou. Chéri. Le Toutounier. Gigi.* Diminutives. Endearments. Baby talk. Books with such names must belong to an inferior genre, must be meant for sentimental young girls and animal lovers. *Dialogues de bêtes* has even been translated as *Creatures Great and Small.* On top of which the author is French, and like all French women, as is well known, seems very expert about love. Even her name, her pen-name, sounds like a pet-name: Colette. There it is, in a nutshell. If you are a serious person, don't bother to read her.

Oh yes, she wrote a lot of books. She must have been like George Sand, about whom a disgruntled lover said that she could turn on the tap at will. Since when have abundance, facility, been a sign of quality? Girls may be early talkers, but, as Freud said, they are just good at imitating: proper little monkeys. It does not mean that they understand what they say. 'Little girls are quick and shallow', Mr Stirling the schoolmaster tells Maggie

1

Tulliver who has just understood a Latin rule. Colette also was quick: she was barely in her twenties, her husband Willy told her to write about her schooldays, and there was *Claudine at School*. All down on paper.

That was very much the image of Colette I grew up with. I use it as a starting-point, because, surprisingly, it is still pervasive, despite her growing reputation, and the wealth of editorial, biographical and critical material that has recently poured out about her. Debates remain cluttered by assumptions and prejudices you would not have to deal with if she was called, simply, Léo Colette as her musician brother was.

Colette? For me, then a French adolescent middle-class girl, she was the author of *Gigi*, a film with Leslie Caron, fanciful and shallow. And of *Claudine at School*, a disturbingly crude if witty book. And of the daring *The Ripening Seed*, which I was not allowed to read. It made the grown-ups chortle knowingly, and say that Edwige Feuillère had been wonderful in it. In any case, Colette belonged to an inferior caste, she had been the friend of silly poets like Paul Géraldy, for whom I felt much contempt. Cocteau might also have been her friend, but Cocteau had always been over-catholic in his tastes, that came from his own – shsh, you know. I had seen a film about Colette, and been struck by a disparity between the image of Colette that I had, and the haunted eyes of a formidable and evidently much respected fat old woman. But I had been repelled by dyed hair and abundant make-up; there was an old woman married to a positively servile, much younger man. That showed how dreadfully immoral she must have been. You did not do such things. You could not take such a person into account, especially when she wrote about frivolous feminine things, love and plants and animals and her family. I had been taught to admire superior male topics, things to do with politics and philosophy. 'Woman is natural, therefore abominable,' Baudelaire had written. You had to cleanse yourself of that original female sin. Become a 'filse',* a son–daughter who so thoroughly adopted patriarchal values that she became worthy of the male inheritance. Real literature was about mind and anguish and nothingness and night, white or black. It spoke of the absurd and of role-playing, class-warfare, neo-colonial guilt and existence and essence. You became worthy to the extent you could formulate abstract thoughts. You proved your seriousness about life by saying striking things about death. I was nothing if not a good monkey. I dedicated years to demonstrating my seriousness. My ignorance of Colette remained perfect.

'Don't tell me you haven't read *Sido!*' a friend exclaimed a few years ago. 'But it's magnificent.' 'Colette, my mother-in-writing,' another friend called her. I began to read Colette. I was bowled over. I was crucified with shame, thinking I must have seen that prose, and not perceived how beautiful it was. Talking enthusiastically about my new discovery, I also, chasteningly, perceived that it wasn't exactly a discovery... France and the United States, in particular, were (almost) swarming with good books. The fifteen-volume Flammarion edition was being replaced by a three-volume one, the Pléiade were bringing out a richly annotated Colette also, scores of paperbacks existed, and practically all of the works had been translated into English, although the translations were more currently available in the States than in England. There were lives, monographs, essays,

---

*This is the term used by Antoinette Fouque to say that the daughter wants to be her father's son rather than her mother's daughter – or her father's daughter, for that matter.

photograph albums, editorial studies... it was almost overwhelming. But it was my own dialogue with Colette I wanted to recount. Ashamed of my hostile and prejudiced ignorance, immersed for months in Colette studies, and in Colette's own works, I had so wanted to yield, be taken over. I mourned that I hadn't been, wasn't, more like her. I was saved from conversion by remembering how little time she had for conversions. She had told how her mother had gone to see the vicar, to protest about the way the children were being indoctrinated by catechism. The way they were being taught to ask questions about life. She had come back delighted with some rare plants the vicar, a keen gardener like herself, had given her.

* * *

That Colette was a woman writer made a double difference. French women writers were studied very little when I was at school and university, and so far as I could see, they were still being read very little in English schools and universities. Subtle suggestions were made: Mme de Staël was immoral and overbearing; nobody need bother read her novels which were solemn and out of print anyway, but her critical works about the German Romantics (all male) were all right. The same, more or less, applied to George Sand, but it was her pastoral novels that were still being read, strictly by children. *La Princesse de Clèves*, by Madame de La Fayette, which was about not doing it, was the only one of her works to be mentioned, and held to be a high-flying classical delicacy. The odd love sonnet by Louise Labé, or melancholy letter by Mme du Deffand, were 'in' – in anthologies. Actually, come to think of it, letters were 'in' more than anything else when it came to women writers, the most 'in' of the lot being Mme de Sévigné. We were force-fed her letters to her daughter, and I developed the unformulated notion that women writers were petty and over-protective. As for Colette, she was both trifling and immoral: out, out, out. She may have written plenty of letters, and not a few inside her books. She may have written about her mother's letters, in *The Break of Day*. We did not know this, and in any case she was not regaling her daughter with respectful anecdotes about the King's court, nor writing feelingly about her daughter's tummy-aches.

A parody, but with much truth to it. My (Catholic) school was about making us into dutiful wives and good mothers. University was about making us into mainstream intellectuals and teachers, perpetuating the great, male, tradition. Neither had much time for women writers, and none for Colette. That, in itself, was significant. In her lifetime Colette had always had a large readership, but it had always been non-institutional, and included a high proportion of women who were not academic. Famous 'intellectuals' had always kept their distance. Her recent, remarkable rise in fame, which had started with the centenary year of her birth, 1973, and had gained much impetus from the re-publications and re-readings of women writers of the past brought about by the women's movement in France and Anglo-Saxon countries, had split Colette in two. She had been treated as a deserving case for long overdue scholarship, a case like any other. Or she had become a cause to be pleaded, a *woman*'s cause, though it was recognized that she had never been interested in -isms, had never been political, never a feminist, never made theoretical pronouncements. No equivalent to *A Room of One's Own* in her work, let alone to *Three Guineas!* Still, the camps were drawn, labels bandied about, if not by a

particular critic, at least by her enemy. Your reading of
Colette was 'feminist' if it argued that she had been
'exploited' by her first husband, Willy (which was true)
and that she had had many women friends, and some
women lovers (which was also true). You rescued
Colette from the feminists – poor thing, so much in need
of rescue – if you showed that Willy had been instrumental in her becoming a writer (which was true) and
that she had loved several men, and had had many men
friends (which was also true). Poor Colette indeed, who
had so hated dichotomies, either/or. Who had never
written a single book with a *dual* title.*

Colette's specificity is what is most difficult to speak
about. All we have are traditional concepts and methods.
They may be modernist, but theory goes on producing
either/or: the 'semiotic' *or* the 'symbolic'. You are in the
camp of men *or* in the camp of women. You write about
Colette as a scholar *or* in a subjective, intuitive, manner.
It is difficult to escape from received categories. Colette
deserves that we try. Since I am trying to 'think' about
her work rather than write a piece of fiction inspired by
it, I have to take theory into account, keep my distance.
But she herself was suspicious of ideas. She boasted she
had never had any general ideas to a journalist who was
questioning her about her political opinions. Ideas are in
the third person, they offer themselves as 'objective'. To
have any chance of saying anything relevant about
Colette, I must face up to her as I am, for what I am
worth. Thus I start from what I can deduce from my
experience of Colette. I note that my failure to read her
when I was young had to do with her being perceived as
in a category apart, as a 'woman writer' whose life and

---

*With the exception of *The Pure and the Impure*, which is the replacement title of
Ces Plaisirs..., and has traditionally baffled critics.

work were thought to be educationally dangerous for a young girl meant to become a particular kind of woman. And that the continued ignorance was because her 'womanly' ways were thought to be inimical to the social and intellectual values institutions were passing on to me. The message is crystal clear. I must ask, what difference does it make that she was a *woman* writer?

Part I
The Domestic Circle

Chapter One

The Domestic Circle

Well and good. But where do I start? Refusing dichotomies, stressing the term *woman* writer, suggests that a different order should be found. Different from what?

The first striking thing when you start looking at the work on Colette is the high proportion of biographies that exist. I bet that if you were to look at the percentage of biographical studies to criticism in various writers, Colette would turn out to have the highest number of 'lives'. Not only that, but she would also turn out to have the highest number of photograph albums. There are some perfectly valid reasons for this. She did have a fascinating, and varied, life. Lives, one should say: there is the life as the village child in an idyllicly happy household; the years of the marriage to bullfinch-bellied Bluebeard Willy in decadent Paris and the writing of the *Claudine* novels under his tutelage and name; then the period as the lover of lesbian Missy, alias the Marquise de Belbeuf, and the career as a music-hall mime. Then comes the passionate marriage to baron Henry de Jouvenel, the birth of a daughter, journalism during the First World War and a period as a wife and mother and society hostess. Then the break, the affairs with very young, or younger, men, the more serene years with, and eventual marriage to, Maurice Goudeket; and the ageing, consecrated literary figure ensconced at the heart of Paris, in the Palais-Royal; and the national funeral. The little lady with the triangular, cat-like face and the striking eyes carved out several careers where others would have made do with one, and hundreds of photographs have survived of her various embodiments. As one reads through the biographies or leafs through the albums, one can indulge in many types of fascination. With the exquisite round limbs and mysterious face, with the woman who, like Pater's dream of the Mona Lisa, was all women in one, the secretive lover who knew all forms of passion, the grand old lady of belles-lettres, tough but, oh, so wonderfully 'feminine'.

We never pause to think what assumptions lie beneath our responses. No comparable photograph albums of men writers have survived, and had they done so, would we indulge in the same reveries in front of images of Proust and Gide as we do in front of Colette? Certainly, neither danced semi-naked on stage: but do we read Colette in a different way from them because she did? Do we bring to her photographs, or to the chronicles of her 'amours' with her adolescent stepson, the awareness that we are interested *because* she was a writer? Don't we allow the images and the details of the life instead to be naturalized? Do we not forget that she had been trained in self-advertising and the projection of images by her master publicist of a first husband, Willy, and that she used her training to wonderful effect forever after? And just as we forget how much artifice, and art, went into the production of the images, so keen are we to relate to a beautiful, passionate woman, as a piece of nature, just so we assume that she wrote so wonderfully about nature, and love, because it must have welled up spontaneously in her: we make her into the thing itself. And yet it took decades of craftsmanship and hard graft for her to reach the stage when she could write *The Break of Day*, or *Flore et Pomone*.

Similar types of confusion seep into most of the biographies. Indeed, interestingly, most of the biographers have been women – and a higher proportion of the authors of critical books have been men. It's not just the worrying question of women being yet again in the business of producing material for the theorizing male critics to analyse: biography as 'facts', or 'nature'; criticism as mind. It is that all the biographers, necessarily, transfer elements of themselves into the 'life' they produce.[1] There are personal things at stake for all of them, and the kinds of battle they may carry against previous biographers are the sign of this. The last of them, Geneviève Dormann, for instance, conducts a virulent guerilla war against those she regards as 'feminist' interpreters of Colette. As a result, we have a number of Colettes: the provincial in Paris, the woman who couldn't find love and the woman who did nothing but love, the epicure, the vagabond, the woman who fought for freedom, the immoralist, the model of womanhood. That is fine: anyone who writes a life, or indeed writes about a writer, becomes proprietorial in their reading. What is wrong is that only the best are prepared to acknowledge that they have personal stakes in the matter. The others claim they are writing 'the' objective truth, the latest, best documented (ergo, 'truest') account. Yet, sometimes with the zeal of the hagiographer, they offer the reader an opportunity to identify with 'their' Colette; i.e. to some extent, themselves. It is a relief to turn back to reading Colette, and have the text gleefully, gracefully, bounce back. Then you remember that the reasons why you are interested in her is that she was a writer, and that it is because the way she had with plants, and animals, and flesh, was translated into beautiful prose that you care about it.

And yet... there seems to be a closer interrelation between Colette the woman who lived and Colette the woman who wrote than there is even between Proust the man and Proust the writer. I mention Proust because he is comparable: he also wrote about virtually nothing but his life, as Colette did. But his practice was retrospective, his work, very much one. She wrote sixty or seventy books, over a period of over fifty years, and each book she wrote was geared, ever more subtly, to the period of her life in which she was writing. Each became 'autobiographical' in a different way, but one which always combined a mixture of bold directness and secrecy, openness and 'pudeur' – modesty of a wild and tenderly protective kind. The openness itself of course is generally a front, a cunning pretence, but it does invite biographical reading. The secrecy also invites to it, in that it calls for interpretation, and the biography seems the most obvious place to root it in. And so I think that whoever thinks about Colette finds himself, or herself, shuttling between the life and the works. But perhaps the toing and froing ought to be inspired by something more than a one-to-one relation. Perhaps the patterns of desire, and self-projection, and the quest for the self in and through language, ought to enter into it. Not that I wish to psychoanalyse Colette. I would find that rather dull, but also inappropriate, in that one of the things I find interesting in her writing is that it seems to me to subvert too neat a classification between the ego and the subconscious, for instance. She got her act together at a pretty early stage, and her superego seems to me to have been of an embryonic kind. But that does not mean that psychoanalytic concepts are not helpful.

It may be the first thing that could be said to be typical of her practice, and specific: that the life, and the works, flow into each other more than they do in other writers. It is a proper thing to say, once you have struggled through naturalizing illusions about Colette. There are continuous interferences between the author-as-real-person-in-life, and the author-as-narrator. Between the characters as *alter egos* of the author (like Claudine, or Renée, or Léa), and the author-as-actress of her own fiction: Colette pretended to be Claudine in town; she acted her Renée and her Léa on stage, in her own dramatization of the novels. Gide never went on stage to act the Immoralist or Lafcadio. I mention Gide as a writer whose practice of autobiography and fiction is particularly cunning and inventive. Conversely, Colette wrote a great deal about a character called Sido, which was her mother's name, and a woman very much like her mother. Aragon did something similar with Elsa, and Jouhandeau with his wife Elise. That is, write semi-fictitiously about a real person, called by her real name. But Colette's practice is larger, more consistent and also more varied than theirs. I suppose that if Lawrence had called Ursula and Harriet, and others, 'Frieda', that might have been comparable to what Colette did with Sido.

Something else stands out as specific in Colette; something so often taken for granted in women writers, that it is almost impossible to see. Her entire work, however large its social range, takes place inside what could be called the domestic circle.

'Damn and blast!' my feminist reader exclaims in disgust. 'Did we have to have alluring promises of "something specific" to fall back into the same old rut? Colette was "feminine" because she wrote about woman's estate? What a fine liberation, which makes her whom André Maurois called the "first woman to have written as a woman" stay inside a circle partly devised, and certainly tightened, by the rise of the bourgeoisie, the division between public and private!' And my 'New Right' reader – if I have one – might say, rubbing his hand, 'At last you have seen the light which Colette never lost sight of. Women are womanly when they write of womanly things, know their place, which is home. Colette had the nous not to meddle in manly matters. As for the talk about "feminine writing", it's a lot of bullshit, anyway. Just a question of the subject-matter.'

I would, not very humbly, beg to differ with both commentators. The notion that women writers write domestic, intuitive stuff is a recent one, based upon misreadings of Virginia Woolf, on the vogue of stream-of-consciousness writing, and on simplifying versions of Jane Austen. Nearly all Victorian women writers wrote about public issues, industrial towns, Reform Bills. And they had no qualms about 'realistic' representation. Mme de Lafayette wrote about the court of Louis XIV in ferociously lucid terms. Mme de Staël took on Napoleon I, George Sand fought every political and social battle. So do, today, in their varied ways, Hélène Cixous, Monique Wittig, Marguerite Duras, Jeanne Hyvrard, Simone de Beauvoir. Marguerite Yourcenar writes historical/philosophical novels of admirable scholarship, with male heroes to boot. Not so Colette. Yet nothing is further from her than stream-of-consciousness. She denied the public–private division. She denied the current hierarchies, which made holocausts important while a drive in a forest was not. *La Paix chez les bêtes,* written after Colette had spent time in Verdun close to daily bombardments, visiting a husband who fought through the entire war, ends up with the tale of a car forced to a halt by unhurried pheasants crossing the road. There is every lesson in their gait: 'Let me be. Give me time. *Attendez...*'

Colette used the domestic circle, its diastole and systole, as a heart whose beats enabled her to gather, and irrigate, the entire world. She certainly worked on substituting the circulation that is in that image for the barrier between the home-that-is-your-castle and the big, dangerous world.

In–let us say prudently–'a great deal' of 'modern' fiction and autobiography, the initial family (parents/children, brothers/sisters) serves as a point of departure from which the protagonist moves on to higher things: to seek for selfhood, love, fulfilment, and sometimes to found a new family and have a career. Or the protagonist fails: ever so many novels are about staggering on the threshold, choosing ostracism or alcohol or suicide or art as alternatives to creating a new, domestic circle. Simone de Beauvoir won't repeat the infinite series of grey little boxes in which her mother is trapped: she chooses literature instead of marriage. Gide's Immoralist finds his way which destroys his wife; Roquentin–Sartre or Proust-the-Narrator find their way and choose writing. Childhood, and the childhood house, are something which is in the beginning, as lost paradise or as doom, something you may never get over but which you may also find salvation in recapturing. But, in *Combray* as in *Great Expectations*, as in *The Mill on the Floss*, as in Rousseau's *Confessions*, childhood and the childhood place, whatever you may be doing with it, are something which has to be left behind for the writing to take place. And it is right, at least inevitable, that the initial structure should be transcended. Indeed, come to think of it, the *only* text I can recall that remains within the cyclical, ever-repeated focus of the domestic, and manages to give it cosmic and metaphysical properties, is *Wuthering Heights*. The novel never moves away from the circle created by the tension between high and low, ancient and modern, the Heights and the Grange. Even at the end, when the Hareton–Catherine couple move to the Grange, the Heights remain haunted by the archetypal couple, Heathcliff and Catherine.

The connection with Colette is bizarre, but it deserves thinking about. There is nothing in common, temperamentally or in terms of experience, between the rooted, sternly passionate, short-lived Emily, the author of one major work, and the Vagabond who left her native Burgundy when she was twenty to become a celebrated Parisian, who lived to be over eighty, had an infinitely varied life, a great fund of sensuality, irreverence and what to the Vicar's daughter would have been arrant immorality. Yet there is that thing in common. Imaginatively, in terms of the forms they forged, both women remained in the domestic circle. Domus: home, household. They remained in it because they dared be so thoroughly subversive in relation to it that their very stasis, dramatically in Emily, gently, almost casually in Colette, shook the pillars of the system that makes home what it is in the modern western world: guarantees that it is separate from streets or village or art or politics. With all her apparent nonchalance, there is something mythic and revolutionary in the way Colette rewrote the terms of domestic experience. And so it is from inside that circle that we must look at what she did. After all, what else but domestic trouble befalls the kings and queens of Greek tragedy?

Chapter Two

Phynance

'Quick, quick, my child, there isn't a *sou* left in the house.'
(Willy to Colette)

Home starts with cash. You can't found a new hearth without money. Colette's parents had had money. Sido had been a wealthy widow. Colette didn't start off quite so well.

'Phynance': that is what Jarry's King Ubu, a grotesque compendium of the horrors of the bourgeois, calls money. Finance laced with the 'Ph' of philosophy or the 'Phy' of physics. Ubu's glee at wringing down to the last penny of his victims, nobles and peasants alike, is extreme: then down the trap they go! Colette managed to get a ticket for the famous 'première' of *Ubu Roi*, when the audience were thrown into fits of outrage by Ubu's first word, 'Merdre', 'Shrit'. Thereafter, she always held to her right to say 'merdre', and on occasions resorted to the good king's word to represent her own permanent cash-flow problem: 'See how phynance always goes wrong with me.'[1] And when, in *My Apprenticeships*, she described beautiful Otero's recipe for wringing gold out of a man, perhaps a memory of Ubu's methods crossed her mind:

> 'You look a bit green, my girl,' she once said to me.
> 'Don't forget that there is always a moment in a man's life, even if he's a miser, when he opens his hand *wide*...'
> 'The moment of passion?'
> 'No. The moment when you twist his wrist.'
> 'She added: 'Like this,' and made a screwing movement with her two clenched hands. You seemed to see the blood flow, the juice of fruits, the gold, and goodness knows what else: to hear the bones crack. Can you picture me twisting the miser's wrist? (*My Appr*: 14)

Money makes the world go round... Diamonds are a girl's best friend... Not very romantic to start from there, but that is where writing started for Colette. King Ubu and beautiful Otero make a good godfather and godmother for this particular baby. If Colette begins her account of her apprenticeship to become a writer with the anecdote concerning Otero, and moves on to her own Ubu, Willy with the rotund belly, ready to wring money out of his own missis, this must be because she is equating two kinds of liquidities, which were to be with her always: money and writing. If she hadn't needed to make money by writing, and if she hadn't discovered, thanks to Willy's entrepreneurial energy, that she could make money by writing, it is quite possible she may never have written. She never had £300 a year, and she never had a room of her own in which to write: the provincial in Paris that she was, lived the life of a nomad in the capital, constantly moving from flat to flat. It was years before she had her own place. Even at the time of the affluent rue de Courcelles apartment, when the

Claudine novels were bringing in plenty, Willy arranged for her to have a 'squirrel's cage' in which to do gymnastics: but she had to write in a corner of the bedroom, facing a wall. On top of which, she'd only gone to primary school, and the last thing that would have occurred to her was to want a career as a novelist.

The alternative was simple for a middle-class girl at the end of the nineteenth century. It was marriage or, if your father left you well-off, a comfortable spinsterhood. To get married, you needed a dowry. If your family had become impoverished and could not provide the dowry, things got tough. You only got a husband if you were pretty, and lucky – or clever. The jobs you could get were scarce. If you had the looks, and knew how to look after yourself, and had made the break from your family, you could become 'richly kept', as my grandmother used to put it. This is what Luce, the girl in love with Claudine in *Claudine At School*, does. In *Claudine in Paris*, she meets an old gent and takes it from there. This is also the fate that is being prepared for Gigi by her experienced grandmother and great-aunt. The sky was the limit for successful courtesans of the *belle époque*, as beautiful Otero, who was Edwards VII's mistress, or Liane de Pougy, who married Prince Ghika and made an edifying end, show. *Chéri* is peopled by women like Léa and Charlotte who've done very well. But hundreds must have failed for the few who succeeded. Those who failed eked out a living in the chorus at the opera, like Gigi's mother. Lived and died improvident, in alternately splendid and wretched circumstances, like so many of Colette's characters – Mitsou, Gribiche, Jadin in *The Vagabond*, or Lucette in *Chance Acquaintances*. An impoverished young bourgeoise brought up in the countryside, like young Colette, could 'go up' to Paris like Luce, and try her luck. Sido, her mother, rescued her at least once from the fascination of a married man: the teenager had gone to stay with the man and his family, Sido suddenly appeared and, without a word of explanation, took her away. Some of Colette's later writing shows how great the danger must have been. In *The Tender Shoot*, mother and pubescent daughter strike up a strangely warring alliance against that dangerous seducer, the ageing Don Juan: there is something of a retrospective vengeance in the ferocity with which they drive him away.

Alternatively, a penniless girl who wanted to remain respectable could, in that heyday of the Third Republic, when schooling had become compulsory and free, become a schoolteacher. This is the career for which some of the older girls in *Claudine At School* are preparing themselves. The schoolteachers, Melle Sergent, Melle Aimée, are the Third Republic equivalent to the governesses of Brontë days. Claudine herself is blissfully free from that prospect because her father is well-to-do. Colette's own father was not.

Yet thanks to the farms and lands of 'Le Sauvage', a grumpy middle-aged farmer who had been Sido's first husband, her parents had been well-off. Sidonie Landoy, alias Sido, had been a dowryless young girl herself, visiting Saint-Sauveur-en-Puisaye, Burgundy, when 'Le Sauvage' had seen her, fallen for her and taken her without a penny. She had pined for the lively social and intellectual life she had been leading with her brothers in Belgium, but she had been too sensible not to know which side her bread was buttered. And though 'le Sauvage' had been an alcoholic and violent, she had been a match for him, had thrown a lamp at his face when he had attacked her. He had never done it again. After his timely disappearance, she had been free to marry the dashing Captain Colette, new to the village, and whom she was already in love with. She must have relished her happy union with the Captain all the more for that first marriage.

Captain Colette had had a promising military career brutally interrupted when he had lost a leg at Merignano, during Napoleon III's Italian campaign. Though retired to Saint-Sauver as a tax-collector, he had remained full of dreams and ambitions, but had not fulfilled them. Colette's works tell lovely stories about her father, his attempt to go into politics, his interest in science, in writing, in poetry. Claudine's gently obsessional 'malacologist' of a father owes some of his features to the Captain. The Captain also tried to manage his wife's properties. He did it so badly that the family were ruined, the full extent of the disaster coming to a head when a dowry had to be provided for Sido's elder daughter, Juliette. They had to sell everything, were doomed to never-ending squabbles with the new in-laws. The family house and furniture went, the Saint-Sauveur house with its two gardens where the children had spent such idyllic days. The Captain, Sido and seventeen-year-old Colette moved in with Achille, the elder son, a doctor in Châtillon-Coligny. Which meant that as far as knowing which side your bread is buttered goes, it was extraordinarily fortunate that Henri Gauthier-Villars, a Parisian and man-about-town, handsome, sophisticated and mature, should propose to, and marry, the twenty-year-old girl.

Colette had met him in Paris, where she had gone aged fifteen to accompany her father: he was an old schoolfriend of Henri's father, a distinguished publisher. Henri had a son by a married mistress whom he had been much in love with, and who had died before her divorce was through. Little orphaned Jacques had been entrusted by his father to the kindly Colette family. Henri

must have seen a lot of young Gabrielle – Gabri as she
was then called – on his visits to his son. His motives for
marrying the young girl seem complex. His letters to
friends, recently published,[2] make it clear that he did not
love his 'pretty Colette' anything like the way he had
loved Jacques' mother. But he was captivated. Photographs of the long-tressed secret-looking girl are
evidence of her beauty. The Claudine novels are
evidence of her wit, sexual vitality, and startling
disregard of convention. To the blasé 34-year old
Parisian, who only liked very young girls anyway,
Gabri's lack of sophistication, her mixture of ardour and
innocence, what she will later describe as her own
craving for corruption, must have been appealing
indeed. He must also have felt beholden to the whole
Colette family for their kindness to his son, have dreamt
of making an 'ending' the usual Balzacian way, where
ageing blades marry an unspoilt young virgin. His family
certainly thought he was making a big mistake in
marrying a penniless girl, especially when his own
financial situation as freelance man-of-letters was
precarious, to say the least.

And a big mistake it must have seemed to Willy,
Henri's pen-name, when, the newly-weds being in-
stalled in one set of gloomy rooms after another on the
Left Bank, he had to multiply his phenomenally diverse
fund-raising activities to make ends meet, not just for
one, but two. The bride, it has been claimed, was not a
very good housekeeper. Colette herself has narrated
how her mother had to buy her a winter coat when she
visited her. Tales of the period all point to a pinched and
cramped bohemian existence, with occasional windfalls.
Willy knew everybody, wrote all sorts. He was best
known for his 'Lettres de l'Ouvreuse', Usherette's
letters, witty, punning, inspired musical reviews that he

produced for years and that spread the gospel according to Wagner, backing the real talents, Debussy, César Franck, ... But one of Willy's most consistent source of funds was his production of books on virtually any topic – history, art, music, discreetly or indiscreetly titillating fiction – by means of 'nègres': hacks.

Baudelaire has a neat little story called, 'How to Pay Your Debts When You Are A Genius'. Hounded by creditors, Balzac gets a 400-franc commission for an article; goes and finds a starving talented young man, who is glad of a 200-franc commission for the same. The young man goes away and writes the article, Balzac signs it, the editor is pleased, and Balzac pockets the difference. Poor old Baudelaire was no good at that sort of thing. But Willy was a master of the art, which was evidently much in practice at the end of the century. The system could be many-tiered. The heroine of Le Képi, one of Colette's late stories, uses 'Marco', a man's name, as her pen-name. She is paid one *sou* a page for writing historical novels. She busily researches early Christians in the Paris libraries, delving deep into circus games and catacombs. The man who commissions her get two *sous* a page, the next one four, and the boss at the top, who signs the book, ten. Marco's only progress at the end of Le Képi (Bouvard and Pécuchet-like) is that she's graduated to two *sous*. The story has a strong autobiographical dimension.

Willy was at the ten *sous* top of the pile. He employed squads of hacks. Some of the books sold well. Still, life was hard. It must have occurred to him one day that his idle young wife might help with the housekeeping instead of pining. She could tell a good story, she had shown in society that her wit could bite. He had married her as the genuine article, the country wife in whom he sensed a native 'rouée'. What about turning it all to profit?

We had been married a year or a year and a half when M. Willy said to me: 'You ought to put down what you remember of your board-school days. Don't be shy of the spicy bits. I might make something of it. Money's short.'

These last words, which were his daily *leitmotif* – a theme developed with unfailing fantasy for thirteen years – alarmed me less than the first. For I had just recovered from a long and very serious illness that had left me sluggish in mind and body. But having found and bought, at a local paper-shop, a number of copy-books similar to those I had used at school, I set to work. Diligently, with complete indifference, perched at the corner of the desk, the window behind me, one shoulder hunched and my knees crossed, I wrote.

When I had finished, I gave my husband a manuscript that was closely-written and did not overrun the margins. He read it through and said: 'I was wrong. It's no use at all.' (My Appr: 22)

Relieved, Colette says, she returned to her divan, her cat, her books. But a few years later, while tidying up some drawers, Willy came up against the forgotten copy-books:

'Hullo!' said M. Willy. 'I thought I had chucked those away.'
He opened one of the copy-books, turned the pages:
'It's rather nice.'
He opened a second copy-book and said no more. A third, a fourth.
'My God!' he muttered. 'I am the bloodiest fool.'
He swept up the scattered copy-books just as they were, grabbed his flat-brimmed top hat and bolted to his publisher's. And that is how I became a writer. (My Appr: 55)[3]

Thus, or so Colette says, *Claudine At School* was born. Its success was huge. Fifteen-year-old Claudine impertinently chronicles the school-life of her native village.

The girls have a peasant knowledge of the realities of life, they spy on the lesbian 'amours' of the headmistress and the sub-mistress, on the inspector who makes passes at all the pretty females he can grab. Willy made Colette follow suit. So came *Claudine in Paris* and *Claudine Married*, where the village girl is confronted by the sophistication and perversity of Parisian life. Later there is *Minne*, Colette's effort to move into more distanced territory with the story of an adolescent girl, narrowly and protectively brought up in Paris, who thinks she is in love with the 'Apaches', the wild bunch of budding gangsters who haunt the fortifications in the vicinity of her respectable home. Willy, keen to see whether Minne didn't have it in her to do as well as Claudine, made Colette write a sequel filled with adulteries, *Les Egarements de Minne*. Colette was gradually to shed Claudine as a snake does a skin. Claudine had such vitality as a character, she had appealed to such a large readership, that she had become a 'type', as Catulle Mendès told Colette. Yet Claudine fades little by little. Her last major appearance is in *The Sentimental Retreat*. That had been preceded by *Claudine and Annie*, whose French title had been, *Claudine s'en va, Claudine goes away*. In effect it had been Annie who had gone away, left her husband: the title was signalling the disappearance of the 'type', though. Claudine flits in and out of *The Tendrils of the Vine*, a familiar whose vitality remains contagious. Then she vanishes for good, to be resurrected in name only in the title of *My Mother's House*, in French *La Maison de Claudine*. That laid the ghost to rest.

What marks the whole period between 1900, the date of publication of *Claudine at School*, and 1906, when Colette and Willy separated, is a riot of publicity, engineered by Willy round the character of Claudine. He made Colette pose as Claudine, twinned by Polaire, a fiery, wasp-waisted *pied-noir* actress who played Claudine on stage. Both girls were dressed in black school-blouse, round white collar, booties, with short hair: Colette's 1.57 m tresses had been cut. Colette also posed for publicity photographs, with a look of knowing innocence, kneeling at master Willy's feet, writing his name on the blackboard, begging with her dog Toby-Chien. With modern advertising genius, Willy exhibited his Claudine, the girl who was supposed to have given him the material for the books he was supposed to have written and that were signed Willy:'"This child has been most precious to me", 'he would say, laying his soft hand on Colette's head. '"She has told me quite delicious things about her board-school"' (My Appr: 55). The name Claudine sold collars and cosmetics. Caricaturists showed Willy as a sculptor lubriciously modelling the clay-figure of his schoolgirl, or as a master-puppeteer pulling the strings of Colette and Polaire. And so, Colette was made to fetishize the character she had created. She prostituted herself, partly through what she wrote, the lesbian stuff having been added as spice at Willy's suggestion, but mostly because she acted as if she were the real thing, Claudine. Interesting, where prostitution is, when it comes to fiction. Willy, cast as 'the author', cast Colette as 'nature', the *oral* source of the *written*, which was supposed to be his province.

In that particular scenario indeed Willy went one better than Pygmalion. He produced not one, but two, Galateas: the fictitious one, who had come to life as his young wife; and the stage one who sprang off the stage, Polaire. He walked his Galateas everywhere. He was their Author. The author of their days. They were his daughters, he called them so, he looked old enough to be their father. They were also the offspring of his brain, they were his actresses (Colette also played Claudine on stage), his pupils in libertinism. He could have it off with the creatures of his imagination, since it was thought they were his wife-and-mistress. Colette has claimed that sometimes he locked her up like a severe schoolmaster, until she had finished her daily imposition, and she has described her condition and that of the other hacks Willy exploited as that of workers in factories. Willy was the master in all those senses too, he held the whip. All the glory of Colette's forced labour went to Willy of the supposedly indefatigable pen. Yet, as the wife, she shared in the financial gains. The couple moved to an elegant flat, rue de Courcelles. They bought a house in the Jura, the Monts-Boucons, which Colette loved and which became Annie's house, in the two novels with Annie.

If we look at things from Willy's point of view, it was a damned clever game he was playing, and his wife was jolly lucky to have such a good manager. His endlessly inventive packaging of the *Claudine* novels, and his ability to keep his name in the public's eye, were instrumental to their success. Colette might have needed shaking up from time to time, but she was playing her role willingly enough, and she too enjoyed the money. It is a boring exercise to try to cast either husband or wife as the villain of the piece.[4] Things were more complicated than that, and what is important about these years in relation to Colette's career as a writer is that Willy made a professional out of her. He taught her the discipline and hard grind of writing, he kept her from the start in touch with a real, a commercial market, he taught her perfectionism in proof-reading. He put her in touch with a tough world of writers and journalists who lived by their pen, and showed her that it could be the source of her income too. And he taught her to produce and control her image. In a period in which middle-class young women associated writing with secrecy, but also with sincerity, pouring out their innermost thoughts onto the pages of private diaries, Colette learned to associate writing with make-believe, the wearing of a mask, a public voice. Her hostility to Marie Bashkirtseff, the author of a diary that was famous in the *fin-de-siècle* and had been made the more moving by her premature death, must have to do with a learnt dislike of naively confessional modes of writing. She preferred Renée Vivien, who had also died young, but had been a poetess, had known about art-as-disguise. Colette was concealing her married misery from her own mother: she was not going to tell the world.

And so, in a period in which *privacy*, in life, in art, in writing, was the motto hanging over women, Colette learnt that writing is *public*. In that, she escaped from the period separation of public and private.

Make-believe and make-up were of the essence of her next career, the music-hall career on which she embarked after her separation from Willy. Of course, she had to earn a living: she had no diplomas, but had been training on the trapeze in her squirrel-cage of the rue de Courcelles, had acted in private performances, and attended Georges Wague's mime classes. But it may be that she went onto the stage for deeper reasons than the need to keep herself. Perhaps, exhibiting her body for money helped her regain the dignity that exhibiting herself as schoolgirl Claudine had stripped her of. Her docility to Willy had been complete. A thirty-year-old woman, she had posed as a libertine's fetishistic dream of an adolescent. She had been a turn-of-the-century Lolita. Which is not to deny the quality of the novels she had written, so much in excess of their voyeuristic potential, uneven, but exquisitely fresh. Besides, she was not a moralist in the conventional sense. She always remained fascinated by the odd, what in *Bella-Vista* she says other people call 'the perverse'. Yet something in her felt tainted by what she had written and done. In later years, she was to write about *L'Ingénue libertine*, the new title for *Minne* and its sequel, with some distaste. But now she was regaining her lost honour. That, entertainingly, meant losing it in the eyes of the world. She began an affair with the Marquise de Belbeuf, a descendant of Napoleon, a celebrated lesbian whose nickname was 'Missy'. She appeared on stage in a 'mimogramme' with Missy, at the Moulin-Rouge. The act was called 'Rêve d'Egypte', and it involved Missy as archaeologist stripping Colette as mummy of her bandages and kissing her on the mouth ... There was an uproar, respectable members of Missy's high-class circle as well as Willy and his new wife Meg being conspicuous in the audience. Even the Egyptian Embassy protested, and the act had to be re-named 'Songe d'Orient', and Missy replaced by Wague.

The body that had been disingenously exhibited as that of Claudine, made to speak of its pleasures in the falsely ingenuous voice of Claudine, was now being paraded for what it was worth, half-naked, but shielded by powder, speaking with its own movements and suppleness. Colette was in control of the show. She worked to produce her own acts. She was no longer faking naturalness (pretending to be Claudine) to support an artistic production (the *Claudine* novels) of which she was being robbed as author. It makes sense that the novel she produced in this period, *The Vagabond*, and its sequel, *The Shackle*, should be her most unguarded. Authoriality is cleansed from its link with a supposedly natural body. She now found that she could earn a living with her pen without having to prostitute her talent, or her image: the novels were successful, *The Vagabond* got three voices for the Goncourt prize. Self-expression, for Colette, had become compatible with being self-supporting.

Repeatedly in after years, Colette claimed that she hated the misery of writing. Had it not been for the good habits enforced upon her by Willy, her natural indolence and taste for life might have prevailed, and she might have stopped writing. But financial need took over from Willy as a hard task-master. Even when Colette began to earn a decent living with her books, even when, around 1910, journalism began to provide a regular income, when, in 1912, Colette had married a high-class high-powered second husband, a baron, the owner of a castle, the editor of *Le Matin*, Henry de Jouvenel, even then, his grand style of living, political ambition and lack of a sufficient personal fortune meant that he needed a wife who could find plenty of money. To that second marriage as to the first, Colette had brought no dowry but her talent. True, she was more affluent than she had been, her reputation was growing. She owned Rozven, a house in Brittany by the sea, which Missy had given her, and which she did not take back, though Colette had left her for Jouvenel. But insecurity for Colette remained around the corner. She loved filling her house with friends. She shared her husband's expensive tastes. He left her in 1923, because the marriage had broken down, through his repeated adulteries, because Colette's unconventional behaviour and 'scandalous' past ill-served the interests of a politically ambitious man, and most dramatically, because he had discovered that his wife was having an affair with his adolescent son from a first marriage, Bertrand. Yet it was *phynance* which perhaps had the largest share in the separation. For Jouvenel's next wife, Madame Dreyfus, brought him the huge and secure fortune that Colette's literary earnings could not hope to emulate.

Colette's third union, with Maurice Goudeket, whom she met in 1925 and married in 1935, brought her even less financial security. It was the years of the Great Depression. Goudeket's business ventures floundered or never took off for long. Colette was so keen to escape from the treadmill of writing that she tried to launch a beauty salon in 1931. It was a commercial disaster, and threw her back upon writing. Her passion for the 'landscape of the human face' came across more effectually when she made it up in words than with the help of whipped creams and kohl. Léa's struggle with age was better served by the pen that wrote *Chéri* than actress Cécile Sorel's face by Colette's brush and eyeliner. Natalie Clifford-Barney, the celebrated American 'Amazon' and a life-long friend of Colette, is quite entertaining about the way Cécile Sorel and even sweet young Bel-Gazou, Colette's own daughter, came out of Colette's beautician hands looking ten years older than they were. It is worthy of note, though, that all of Colette's attempts to earn a living with something other than her pen were of the traditional, female, kind. They had to do with the body, but also with *display* of the body: as an artefact, by a mime or make-up artist who needed cash.

Colette's literary production is about as 'natural' as that of Walter Scott. The Author of the *Waverley* novels preserved his writing by means of anonymity and pseudonyms. He once compared himself to Harlequin, who could no longer act after he had been foolishly persuaded to remove his mask. 'There is nothing that gives more assurance than a mask' (My Appr: 55), Colette remarked about the *Claudine* novels that were published under the name of Willy. The man's books, Scott's, hide under the absence of a name, or a comedy of false names. The woman's books eventually display a name that parades its own familiarity. It seems to be nature itself. Yet it was arrived at through a process whose complexity is comparable to the extraordinary authorial charade of the *Waverley* novels. The name is Colette.

Chapter Three

The Name of the Father I

Colette. What is that?

It's the feminine diminutive of Colas, or Nicolas. Colin, Coline, Colette. Nicole, Nicolette, Colette.

It is also an ordinary southern surname. It means 'little hill'. Col (pass), Colline, Colette. Colette's father was called Captain Jules-Joseph Colette. He came from Toulon, on the Mediterranean.

If you wanted to go the way of Freud, the area of speculation would be obvious. Little hill, little mound, clitoris, Little Phallus. You might even say, Little Red Riding Hood. Or you might not. You might say, funny, there being such coincidences in life. Or, such coincidences will always sprout, when a mode of speech (like the psychoanalytic) is fashionable.

The woman writer who came to call herself Colette, as if that had been her first, girlish, diminutive name, and she was inviting the reader to share in a special kind of intimacy, was adopting her father's surname as her only name. She was choosing the patronymic. The history of that choice is the history of the kind of writer she became.

In any case, the evolution and habits of the Colette family had much disrupted the traditional distribution of parts between male and female, with their consequences in language: and in particular, passing on of what in French are called 'noms propres', surnames and first names, names for the members of the clan. For instance, Achille, Colette's elder brother, the doctor, was called Achille Robineau, Robineau being the surname of his father, 'Le Sauvage', Sido's first husband. Only, as Sido was already having an affair with Captain Colette at the time of the child's conception, it may well be that his real father was Captain Colette, though he bore the name of the official father. Achille called one of his daughters Colette. Was this because he liked the name, or was he indicating through his naming of his daughter who his real father was? Certainly, the effect is bizarre in Sido's letters to her daughter. For she calls her own husband 'Colette', never Jules nor Joseph, and she also writes about little Colette her granddaughter: she is living in a little house close to her son after her husband's death. The reader has to distinguish between three Colettes: the Captain, the writer, the little girl. Achille had chosen his own daughter to carry on the patronymic. True, he only had daughters, and it wouldn't have worked with a boy, he would have had to call him Jules or Joseph. But the effect wouldn't have been half so great.

I said earlier that Colette's subversion of domestic structures reminded me of *Wuthering Heights*. Cathy: Catherine Earnshaw, Catherine Heathcliff, Catherine Linton. When Mr Lockwood first comes to the Heights, he finds it as difficult to find a traditional locus for Cathy (is she Hareton's wife, Heathcliff's wife?) as the reader of Sido's letters may find it to assign a recognizable status to the name Colette. Emily Brontë's novel has the great merit of showing the structures archetypally. It can help pinpoint what the naturalization of the name 'Colette' had made invisible.

If we apply contemporary theory to the distribution of roles between the father/male and the mother/female, nineteenth-century 'patriarchy' works in the following ways:

1) *The father has power (financial, moral, civil) over his household, especially his wife and daughters, and they owe him allegiance. If he dies, his eldest son takes over, and the allegiance goes to him.*
2) *Father or elder brother have the right of 'exchange' of women in marriage. Women, who are the object of exchange, pass on from the father's house, or the elder brother's house, to that of the husband.*
3) *Inheritance is passed from father to son. The daughter is given away with a dowry.*

The characters in *Wuthering Heights*, and the various members of the Colette family, operate at least nominally within this pattern. Old Mr Earnshaw is the master of the Heights. When he dies, his elder son, Hindley, takes over. Hindley wants his sister Cathy to marry Linton, who is rich (and will take her without a dowry?). Matrimonial exchange makes Cathy pass from the Heights to the Grange. The same contract, later on, makes Cathy II her daughter, pass from the Grange to the Heights. Similarly, Sido, whose father was dead, was married off, dowry-less, to 'le Sauvage', by her elder brothers. When the Colette family were ruined, they moved to the elder son's house, and after Captain Colette's death, it was Achille again who looked after his mother.

But in two respects, there are striking departures

from, or subversion of, this pattern. Having allowed herself to enter into matrimonial exchange, Cathy I falls from the 'Hell' of the Heights to the 'Heaven' of the Grange: she is banished. She has to split, become two people, before she can find peace. Her ghostly self rejoins her primitive double, Heathcliff, and both have one name only: she is called Cathy, he is called Heathcliff. Her daughter, or earthly self, who has been forced to climb into the Hell of the Heights by her marriage to Linton, marries Hareton Earnshaw. Her new name, Catherine Earnshaw, becomes *her mother's name*; and she and her husband go to live in *her* birthplace, the Grange. Her fate is matrilinear in a double sense.

This is ultimately and paradoxically brought about by the way in which Heathcliff savages the entire fabric of patriarchal tradition, through a cunning use of its essentials, matrimonial exchange and inheritance. He despoils Hindley who, as heir, has the right to dispose of the fatherly estate as he pleases. He marries Isabella Linton to get her share of the Linton money. He uses his son Linton as a pawn in the marriage game: he is male, that means he'll have full powers over his wife and her money. He makes Linton therefore marry Cathy II whom he has entrapped, thereby securing her inheritance from her father, Edgar Linton. Thus both the Earnshaw and the Linton estates are in the hands of the interloper, Cathy's satanic double. Even the happy ending still leaves the inheritance in female hands: Cathy II inherits both estates, and it is through marriage to her that Hareton, the normal 'patriarchal' heir, is reinstated.

There is a less dramatic, but for a while at least equally effective gathering of powers in Sido's hands. For a start, she is no more submissive to her first husband, 'le Sauvage', than Cathy I to Edgar Linton: when he tries to beat her in an alcoholic fit soon after their marriage, she throws a lamp into his face, and he remains scarred for life: never beats her again. After his death, she is mistress of his house, of the estate. Like Hareton, Captain Colette became well-off through marriage. Part of Sido's power in the Colette household must have had to do with her financial position, however little she made of it, and however complete her trust in her improvident husband's management. Colette's own access to independence and her 'own', only, name, will be in 1923, with the publication of *Le Blé en herbe (The Ripening Seed)*, when, after having climbed into the hell of Paris through her dowryless and impotent marriage to Willy, and the breakdown of her bewildering second marriage to high-born Jouvenel, she finally decides to use one name only.

4) *The mother produces the child. The father does not produce it, but begets it.*

In an article concerned with women and creation, Antoinette Fouque argues that women do have a privileged access to creation. They are the sex that 'makes' life, produces living beings, children. Only through an amazing distortion can it be said that it is men who 'naturally' or even culturally 'make': books, machines, science, History; while women, when they make those things, 'make as if', imitate male creation. In fact, it is men who 'make as if', 'font comme'. They imitate the production of the living in what they create.[1] They devise analogies between bodily and 'spiritual' creation, to arrogate to themselves the exclusive right to creativity. Thus Montaigne argues that he prefers the offspring of his brain (his Essays) to the offspring of his loins (his daughter). Women have so lost the awareness that they do 'make' that when they attempt to write books or make music, they behave as if they were biologically or 'naturally' deprived of the ability: they become the hysteric Charcot and Freud studied. Or they imitate imitation: imitate man's creation, which itself is an imitation of true production: the production of the living ('production du vivant').

Circumstances, temperament, talent and intelligence so combined in Colette's case that she never lost track of her ability to 'faire du vivant', as a woman.

It is interesting to look at the two versions of creation in Genesis in the light of Antoinette's Fouque's theory. In Chapter I, God says, 'Let there be light ... and there was light'. The act of speech is at one with the act of creation. On the last day, God makes man: 'God created man: male and female created he them.' As speech and creation are one, so there is one human being, though of two genders. But in Chapter II, the one used by Church authorities and the western tradition, creation is split. God is a craftsman, a kind of potter, or sculptor. He 'makes as if'. He moulds clay (out of what? his own creation? the earth? nature?). He then breathes into it, and the breathing, which is not yet speech, animates the clay, produces life, Adam. Then God calls his creation Adam. Later, Adam calls the creatures. And finally, to make a mate fit for Adam, God performs what resembles a caesarean operation. He opens Adam's side, he removes a rib, he makes a woman out of the rib, he bids her obey Adam. She is born 'second', into a world in which things already have a name. And she is born through an operation in which, as with the clay, God makes *form* out of *matter*. In effect, creation has been split into three components: matter, form and speech (breathing, giving names).

God, in Chapter II, has lost his 'female' potential, his ability to 'faire du vivant'. He has to go through a series of dissociated operations. He can neither speak-and-create, nor engender through love. For God to be able to do that, he has to be androgynous, male and female. Indeed, in the marquetry of the stalls in the chapel of the Communal Palace in Siena, representing the verses of the Creed, God is shown pregnant. He contains the Son within a medallion inside his own belly: 'Genitum, non factum; consubstantialem patri.'

The power of the Patriarch in the Bible is bound up with the predominance of the second Chapter, though, which splits form and matter, speech and breathing, and shows man to come *before* woman, and to be a higher being. The right of inheritance is connected with the covenant God makes with (male) man, and depends upon the 'begetting' of sons by fathers ('So and so begat so and so who begat...'). Fathers being sure that they did beget the sons rests upon family structures through which fatherhood can be established, and woman cannot roam.

In terms relevant to artistic creation, elements become distributed between men and women: upon which much theory has been written.

5) *The Father has the Phallus/the Transcendental Signifier. He gives the Name. The Mother lacks the Phallus, and what it organizes she has no direct access to. Woman cannot 'say' (Lacan).*

Some of the cultural distinctions between Father and Mother that ensue could be summarized as follows:

(a) The Name-of-the-Father acts as the guardian and guarantor of language. The woman has only a first name; she takes her father's, then her husband's surname.

(b) The Father bequeaths his name; the Mother has no name to pass on.

(c) The Father is the guardian of the Law, of the Symbolic; the Mother teaches the child to speak.

(d) Fatherhood is what structures culture, it is the Invisible, what cannot be demonstrated 'biologically': it takes an organized family structure for fatherhood to exist.[2] The Father is bound up with the spiritual. The Mother is connected with matter, nature, body, earth, etc. in opposition to form, spirit, etc.[3] Motherhood is self-evident, since the baby can be known to be born from its mother. In modern times, motherhood can also be seen to be linked to tenderness, home, realism... In *Ulysses*, Stephen Dedalus puts it rather well:

'Fatherhood, in the sense of conscious begetting, is unknown to man. It is a mystical estate, an apostolic succession, from only begetter to only begotten. On that mystery and not on the madonna which the cunning Italian intellect flung to the mob of Europe the church is founded and founded irremovably because founded, like the world, macro- and microcosm, upon the void. Upon incertitude, upon unlikelihood. *Amor matris*, subjective and objective genitive, may be the only true thing in life. Paternity may be a legal fiction.' (quoted in Gilbert and Gubar, 1979: 651)

(e) Authorship, and the production of the *written*, is also connected with fatherhood: in most literary texts, Edward Said has argued, the convention is:

that the unity or integrity of the text is maintained by a series of genealogical connections: author – text, beginning-middle-end, text – meaning, reader – interpretation, and so on. Underneath all these is the imagery of succession, of paternity, or hierarchy (quoted in Gilbert and Gubar, 1979: 5)

Woman is the muse, the text is dedicated to her, she can be the *oral* source of the text (as Colette was supposed to be for Willy), the source of inspiration. But certain types of craft, at least in the nineteenth century (following upon the division of labour?), pertain to women, and to story-telling (orality). Thus Nelly Dean sews, while Joseph reads the Bible. She sews whilst she tells the story to Lockwood, who locks it into a written text, wood if not stone tablets.

No doubt it could be shown that the series of oppositions I have summarized, and which surface in so much contemporary debate, are too neat, and that a lot of families did not function that way, even in the nineteenth century. You have to distinguish between countries, periods, classes, town or country. But it is enough to think of a random series of texts, *Dombey and Son*, Mill's *Autobiography, Washington Square, Madame Bovary* or *Eugénie Grandet*, to realize that the dichotomies are significant. Their purpose is to make perceptible the originality, or peculiarities, of the world created by Emily Brontë (but not just her), and of the Colette family.

Let us take Mr Earnshaw. There is the bizarre scene at the beginning of the novel, when on his return from his trip to Liverpool (to the sea), instead of the expected gifts his children and Nelly have asked for, he produces a gypsy child out of the depths of his own great-coat. It is as though, like the God of the Siena chapel, Mr Earnshaw wanted to be a mother: to engender his own child, produce his own fondly loved foundling, who will twin his daughter, become the cuckoo-son to be preferred over his son-and-heir. Is Heathcliff Mr Earnshaw's book, his spiritual offspring, preferable, as to Montaigne, to the offspring of his loins? Heathcliff has one name only, a name that roots him in nature, 'heath' and 'cliff' which are the things Cathy I/Emily loves, and not in socialized fatherhood. Or perhaps Mr Earnshaw is being of the devil's party without knowing it, he delights in subverting his own home, and the patriarchal order he is supposed to prop up. It is worthy of note that the scene has its echo in Charlotte Brontë's *Villette*, where a widowed father also produces a child, a daughter, out of the depths of his greatcoat. And in *The Mill on the Floss*, where Mr Tulliver brings back a *bundle of books* for his daughter Maggie. *The History of the Devil* is among them. In the process of moving into a mothering role, the fathers license their daughters. They give them power. Mr Earnshaw gives Heathcliff to Cathy instead of the *whip* she had asked for. Mr Tulliver gives literacy to Maggie.

There was nothing devilish about Captain Colette. He was brave, he was gallant and out-going. He was gentle, he worshipped his wife, competing with his children for her love. He licensed his daughter; would take her, Colette tells, on his electioneering trips, letting her get quietly plastered at the café afterwards, till Sido smelled the child's breath in the horse-drawn cart on the return from one expedition, and forbade her to go again. The Captain also gave up: 'You've robbed me of my best election agent,' he complained (*My M's H*: 55). Like Mr Tulliver, his 'business' mismanagement ruined his family.

He was a man of startling wit. He had a leg cut off at the battle of Merignano. He insisted on the leg being put by his side on the stretcher. He was visited in hospital by Napoleon III, who found him with his amputated leg swathed in bandages next to him still. Asked the usual, 'And how are we doing?', 'Mother and child are doing well,' he replied.

45

There is strangely more than courage and wit in this. Is it wisdom, hanging on to the amputated limb, allowing himself to become used to its separateness from the body? Does the man feel he's been made female, castrated by the amputation, and is he being cheerfully stoical about it, since he can crack such a joke? Dreadful frustration this otherwise gentle man must have felt. His daughter speaks of the terrible rages she inherited from him, explosive, in which he would crumple and destroy paper, or crack the marble chimney-piece 'with two kicks of his one foot' (*Sido*: 166). It is interesting that, while she recalls the full and musical sound of his voice, comparable to that of 'an angry sea', she can only fully visualize him *sitting* in his arm-chair: otherwise he is a 'wandering, floating, figure, full of gaps' (ibid.: 166–7). One of Colette's stepsons, Renaud de Jouvenel, attributed great weight to the amputation. He wrote to one of Colette's biographers[4] that Colette had always hated men because she had felt repulsed throughout childhood by her one-legged father. I find this hard to reconcile with the tone with which she writes about her father, her memory of the cat-like, secret strength there was in his arms when he tossed her up into the air. Also, she seems to have so loved her brothers, fallen so completely for Willy, then Jouvenel. The remark suggests that what Colette found repulsive in men was their weakness, their being symbolically castrated, which is rather self-contradictory.* And given Colette's relish for life, it seems inappropriate to talk about her being repelled by anything. On top of which, Renaud de Jouvenel had been neglected by Colette in favour of his elder half-brother,

---

*Did she project amputation onto all other men, or resent them for not being amputated?

Bertrand. There may be jealousy and resentment in the remark.

Still, it points to a shady area, and underlines something about the Colette family. The father felt diminished, not just in relation to his well-to-do wife, but because of his lack of mobility, his aborted military career, his forced sedentary life. A 'poet and townsman' exiled to the countryside, he had something exasperatingly 'missing': the folded trouser-leg and crutches were painful evidence of that. In the Freudian/Lacanian terms evoked earlier, according to which the father 'has the Phallus', the absent leg may have been important. Fortunately there is also something very positive about the Captain's ability to play without horror with the 'female' implications of his infirmity. His analogy between his leg and a baby, his 'mothering' of the severed limb, bespeak a mature and tender man. A man who loves women, does not think it is 'horrible' to be reduced to the status of his joke. It is of a piece with his grumbling about the loss of his 'best election agent'.

For a daughter, it must have been immensely creative to have such a father. Not only did he leave her free, give her a sense of her own importance: his own lack created a space for her, as Mr Earnshaw's introduction of his 'baby' into the household produces fulfilment for his daughter.

Catherine Earnshaw I takes all sorts of freedom. To her father's aggrieved: 'Why cannot you always be a good girl, Cathy?', she replies with a: 'Why cannot you always be a good man, father?' She daringly demands that goodness (i.e. quietness) be only required of daughters by good, i.e. virtuous, fathers. Obedience ceases to be a social duty, she links it with moral issues that in their turn threaten the patriarchal order. She writes her diary in the *margins* of the family Bible, grumbling against her tyrant of a brother, recounting days spent with Heathcliff on the moors. Yet the Bible is *the* patriarchal book. Joseph, a parodic surrogate father always reminding others of duty, obedience, the olden days, fire and brimstone, is forever reading the Bible. The Bible is the book which Victorian fathers pass on as an inheritance to their sons. Mr Tulliver, who till then has always favoured Maggie, his 'little wench', gets his son Tom to write his will of vengeance in the family Bible, when he is on his death-bed. But in *Wuthering Heights*, literacy remains on the side of the females. The younger Catherine cherishes her books, mocks Hareton for not knowing how to read. True, it is Hareton's *name* that is on the door lintel, and this is the first script he learns to read, in a first halting bid to assert his stolen mastery of the place. The book however finishes with young Catherine teaching him playfully to read: a reconciliation, a balance, a mutual giving and ownership in the couple that stands for an idyllic, earthly figure.

This suggests new relations between men and women. They are bound up with the strength of character and independence of the women, of Cathy I initially. She, of course, is very much *her father's daughter*. In the Brontë family, also, it was the daughters, not the son, who fulfilled the father's dream of creation, and thus were heirs to him. In *Wuthering Heights*, Cathy I, not Hindley, asks for a whip. Cathy II re-becomes Catherine Earnshaw. In *Shirley*, Shirley is the heiress – she calls herself Captain Keeldar (Kill-dare). And to think that I also have a Captain Colette! Of such stuff are our associations made of.

It was late in life, and after much writing about her mother, that Colette began to reflect upon her father. 'The Captain' (1929) suggests that she owed much to the discreet and passionate man, seemingly on the outskirts of the circle generated by Sido, but more instrumental in his daughter's life than she ever allowed herself to suspect. Perhaps she had taken him too much for granted when she had created Claudine's father, used him too thoughtlessly. The absentminded, gentle, comical scientist allows Claudine full latitude to carry on as impishly as she pleases, and never sees what is under his nose. Colette had kept off afterwards. Minne, and Renée, in *The Vagabond*, and Mitsou and Chéri are all fatherless. Perhaps she had decided to shelter him, keep him secret as she did those who were most precious to her, her animals, her daughter Bel-Gazou. But suddenly, the words of a medium allow the homeless ghost of the Captain at last to descend upon his daughter. 'What do the dead look like?' Colette asks. 'Like the living,' Madame B. replies. Behind Colette, she sees the 'spirit' of an old man sitting, with 'a spreading, untrimmed beard, nearly white, and rather long grey hair, brushed back'. His eyes are so brilliant their gaze cannot be endured:

> 'He's very much taken up with you *at present*.'
> 'Why at present?'
> 'Because you represent what he would so much have like to be when he was on earth. You are exactly what he longed to be. But he himself was never able.' (*Sido*: 181–2)

The words of the medium bring up a memory for Colette. That of a row of volumes bound in boards, with black linen spines, in the highest shelves of the library at home. No author's name, but titles: *My Campaigns*, *The Lessons of '70*, *The Geodesy of Geodesies*, *Elegant Algebra*, *Zouave Songs* (in verse)... After the father's death, one day, Colette's brother called her to see:

The Domestic Circle

The dozen volumes bound in boards revealed to us their secret, a secret so long disdained by us, accessible though it was. Two hundred, three hundred, one hundred and fifty pages to a volume; beautiful, cream-laid paper, or thick 'foolscap' carefully trimmed, hundreds and hundreds of blank pages. Imaginary works, the mirage of a writer's career.

There were so many of these virgin pages, spared through timidity or listlessness, that we never saw the end of them. My brother wrote his prescriptions on them, my mother covered her pots of jam with them ... we never exhausted those cream-laid notebooks, his invisible 'works'. All the same my mother exerted herself to that end with a sort of fever of destruction: ... not in mockery but out of piercing regret and the painful desire to blot out this proof of incapacity. (*Sido*: 182–3)

Colette it was who drew on this spiritual legacy:

I dared to cover with my large round handwriting the invisible cursive script, perceptible to only one person in the world like a shining tracery which carried to a triumphant conclusion the single page lovingly completed and signed, the page that bore the dedication:

TO MY DEAR SOUL,

HER FAITHFUL HUSBAND:

JULES-JOSEPH COLETTE.

(*Sido:* 182–3)

Leaving the blank notebooks to his heirs, whoever those might be, instead of a will for the sons, Captain Colette may not have left security nor a sense of purpose to his family. But he gave them space to be – and that turned out to be infinitely creative for his daughter. All that blank: all that white. But inside books, beautiful books, bound, and with a loving dedication to his wife. The title, the dedication, and the white. Books in love,

books of love, that spoke of the totality of the devotion.
And the disaster of that devotion, or so Sido thought:

> 'What a pity he should have loved me so much! It was his
> love for me that destroyed, one after another, all those
> splendid abilities he had for literature and the sciences. He
> preferred to think only of me, to torment himself for me,
> and that was what I found inexcusable. So great a love!
> What frivolity!' (*B of D*: 127)

The words of the medium reminded Colette of her
father's books at a time in which she had already filled
them. All that space: no need to write in the margins.
'Virgin pages' had been given to the daughter instead of
the demand that she be a good girl. But the white space
had also been protected by the father. He was the cover,
the binding, the invisible tracery, as well as the one who
licensed the girl to write. Only the author's name was
missing. When Colette wrote that story, for six years
she had been using 'Colette' as her only pen-name. She
had given her father's name to the books. No wonder the
Captain's spirit looked pleased.

Chapter Four

My Father's Daughter

I have started with Captain Colette because his importance in his daughter's achievement has been so underestimated. Colette's own confessed blindness in this respect has been imitated by her critics. 'We relate to tradition through our mothers.' Virginia Woolf's statement has been too simply assumed to be true. Things are more complicated than that, even in a writer who has made as much of her mother as Colette. And generalizations should be handled with care. For what do you do with Elizabeth Barret Browning or the Brontës or Madame de Staël, all of whom lost their mothers when they were young, or with George Sand who had such a bad relationship with her mother? Within nineteenth century terms, it might be truer to say that creation seems to flourish in a gifted woman when (a) the father is loving, gentle, unpatriarchal (like Mr Tulliver, M. de Staël, Captain Colette); or, if overbearing, sufficiently absent or subversive to allow his daughter unconventional growth; and (b), when the mother is loving and powerful enough to give her daughter the confidence to be what she wants. But substitutes may exist. The grandmother, or a close bond with siblings, may constitute a protective and secluded matrix in the absence of the dead or inadequate mother. Maggie Tulliver's need for her brother Tom may have to do with the coldness of her mother, and it may also be that the way the Brontë children became 'twinned' (Ann-Emily, Branwell-Charlotte) produced for them something akin to the dead mother.

There was no need for a substitute for Colette. Sido was not just the centre and protective force of the household, she also had a highly original confidence in the opinions she held. Perhaps, orphaned early and, as the elder girl, made to assume responsibilities in her wayward father's household, she arrived early at independence. There was no one to 'form' or contradict her. Perhaps also, being a stranger to Saint-Sauveur, (she was a city girl, she'd been born in Paris, had grown up in Brussels), she felt critically distant from local attitudes. Colette's stories about her mother taking the dog to church, keeping open house for pregnant servants and stray animals, her original stand on matters religious and moral, show forceful independence in the woman who had such values, and the daughter who so held them up.

Sido's values are of a matriarchal kind. It's the only term that will do for them, though anthropologists now tell us that matriarchal societies never existed. Anecdotes scattered throughout Colette's mature works show that Sido had no time for that pillar of culture, matrimonial exchange. The taboo system was, to say the least, etiolated in the Colette clan. Sido cannot understand why her daughter Juliette is leaving her to go and live with a 'gentleman she doesn't even know': 'But, mother, she's married him. – Exactly. What was I telling you?' She thinks the neighbours' daughter who is pregnant should not marry the seducer who has stolen her from under her parents' roof. She should keep the child, and stay with her parents. And sleep with the man, if she needs to. It's not just bourgeois morality and notion of 'honour' that Sido is denying, but the whole system. Man, for her, should not leave his father and mother and become one with his wife. Sido may have been one with her second husband the Captain, but that was because they loved each other, not because there was any virtue in the estate, the civil or religious ceremony.

Above all things, Sido felt at one with her children. *My Mother's House* opens with her call, 'Where are the children?':

> She would scan the thick green clumps and, raising her head, fling her call into the air: 'Children! Where are the children?'
> Where indeed? Nowhere.

The children play at hiding from the mother, but within the safety of the two enclosed gardens. The cry strikes 'the great wall of the barn' and returns to her 'as a faint exhausted echo':

> And all the while, from among the leaves of the walnut-tree above her, gleamed the pale, pointed face of a child who lay stretched like a tom-cat along a big branch, and never uttered a word. (*My M's H*: 25)

This could be seen as an alternative to Freud's famous scene, developed by Lacan in his reflections on 'the mirror-stage'. The baby-boy plays at throwing away a spool and pulling it back, saying 'fort' (gone), then 'da' (there). He goes on to play with his image in the mirror, making it disappear ('fort') and appear ('da'). Thus, Freud tells us, the child who suffers from the mother's appearances and disappearances, learns a playful control over absence, and also the structuring rudiments of language, the absent/present 'fort' and 'da'. Thus also, Lacan adds, he learns to recognize himself as a 'gestalt', an image, and to recognize self as 'other'. He passes from the 'Imaginary' to the 'Symbolic'. It is a foundation scene, much of which has been made to establish structural links between language, socialization, the development of the psyche. And parallels between the couple absence/presence and the existence of taboos: permitted/forbidden.

The foundation scene in Colette is radically different. It is the children who play at being absent themselves, and the mother is omnipresent, indeed there is nothing that can be more relied upon than her presence. There is some strange cruelty in the way the children make themselves disappear from the mother's gaze like Cheshire cats. Indeed, at the beginning of *My Apprenticeships*, even before the baptism of gold of 'la belle Otéro' and of Willy, there is a dimly evoked similar scene where a little girl, wickedly, pretends to be deaf to her mother's anguished call. The motif must be very deep for Colette to have used it twice at the beginning of 'autobiographies'. But in *My Mother's House* what is stressed is that the children's game takes place within the safety of the garden. They are contained by the mother, within constant hearing of her call. Perhaps she knows that they hear. Her grumble, her cry, 'Where are the children?' will go on ringing in their ears, will make them feel permanently bound to that unanswered call. There will be no world of language that, being 'symbolic' or to do with the 'law', taboos, the mother's absence, would demand of them that they step outside the bounds of the mother's visible or invisible presence. The line of division does not begin to exist, the world of the mother never becomes limited by walls, the domestic circle as something enclosed never materializes. And so, even when Juliette, who has married and has fallen out with her mother, is giving birth, the cries of her labour reach Sido who is out in her garden, waiting:

> Then I saw my mother grip her own loins with desperate hands, spin round and stamp on the ground as she began to assist and share, by her low groans, by the rocking of her tormented body, by the clasping of her unwanted arms, and by all her maternal anguish and strength, the anguish and stength of the ungrateful daughter... (*My M's H:* 85)

Sido fights the 'law' wherever she finds it. She allows her children to be taught no dogma. She gets annoyed by the catechism they're taught, the questions they're made to answer. She dislikes questions. When inquisitive little Colette plies her with them, she becomes exasperated. She must know implicitly that asking questions is getting away from the mother. It is what Oedipus does, when he confronts the oracles. If you can answer the Sphinx's questions you're on your way to incest and parricide. But this is because the taboo's been set up in the first place. Hermeneutics is a male concern, bound up with genesis, with patriarchy, you might argue: Sido doesn't, not in these terms. What she does is what Colette writes she does, and what I say here is interpretative. But it is true to say that Sido seems to feel that knowledge, or certain kinds of knowledge, are the enemy of the mother. The Indo-European root 'gn', on which '*kn*owledge' is based (*gn*ossos, *c*onnaissance), as well as all the words connoting ge*n*eration, is also connected with *knee*, *genou*: because, philologists tell us, the *father* recognized his child by sitting it on his knee. 'On that mystery is the church founded,' as Stephen Dedalus says . . .

What need is there for a daughter with a mother like Sido to be troubled about the mystery of origins? Origins have a skirt fragrant with citronella, origins feed you, and the spider that floats down from the ceiling to sip at the hot morning cup, with chocolate. Sido's own father was a chocolate manufacturer. Slabs of chocolate were left to dry on the house roof at nights, and in the mornings they would bear the imprints of the paws of marauding cats. What you eat is what shelters you. And unlike the Hansel and Gretel story, there is no ogress in hiding. Inside and outside there is nurture, toleration of vagrancy.[1]

And so, from a created world that repudiated current notions of inside and outside, Sido did not just fight exogamy – would not give up her children to husbands and wives – she positively flirted with endogamy, was fascinated by the possibilities of incest. Thus in an episode from *My Mother's House*, Sido tells little Colette repeatedly that she is just 'like my father's daughter'. Then she asks, 'Do you know who my father's daughter was?' – 'Yourself, of course,' the child replies. 'Not so,' Sido explains. One day her father, a great philanderer, came in, carrying a baby girl in his coat. He told little Sido, the eldest girl, that here was a daughter for her, his daughter. She, Sido, was to bring her up. Little Sido first remodelled the baby's ten fingers to make them more 'tapered', more to the father's taste. The doctor could never understand how the baby could develop a digital inflammation in all ten fingers at once. Later, Sido added, she came to cherish the little girl. She looked after her tenderly – and that is whom little Colette is like.

Sido's father behaves like Mr Earnshaw and Mr Tulliver: he becomes a mother, he produces his own baby out of his coat as a rival to the legitimate children within the household. His daughter Sido feels it to be so. Just as Hindley tries to destroy Heathcliff, beating him mercilessly, so Sido remodels the baby's fingers in an operation that has something of a vengeance in it. 'Ah, you like her better than me, do you? I'll show you what I do with your gift.' There is also something of Chinese foot-binding in this tapering of the baby's finger-tips. 'Let us maim this baby-daughter so she can be desirable for the man – the father – and let us seduce the father by means of this.' But then, her aggressiveness appeased by her vengeance, and her getting away with it, little Sido enjoys another kind of pleasure. In what is the fulfilment of what in Freud is fantasy, she is given a baby by her own father (a penis? does it have to be the penis?). She, a little female, is made complete, grown-up, through early motherhood. Sido somehow knows this, and goes on fulfilling that image of completeness through her own daughter. If little Colette is Sido's father's daughter – a kind of Cathy II* or Ligeia, being so like the first little girl, and beloved like her – then she is the offspring of the uncensored female's dream. No taboo has prevailed, or even begun to operate, since it is Sido's own father who gives her the child. This makes the Captain into a surrogate father. And he was actually called Joseph!

It would be untrue to call Sido a 'phallic mother', however powerful she was, for her power had nothing to do with wearing the breeches, or emulating any male characteristics, but came from her confidence in her own

---

*Let us not forget that Cathy II looks remarkably like her mother, and ends up being called Catherine Earnshaw, the surname being her grandfather's.

motherliness, and her lack of self-censorship. Her fascination for incest was stronger than her learnt disapproval. The lovely story, *Le Sieur Binard (The Patriarch)* makes this clear. Achille as a young doctor is called to deliver the child of the youngest daughter of a forester called Binard, who lives in a secluded cottage. The girl is not yet fifteen, and her two sisters also have babies. Beautiful robust babies. Achille is shocked, surprised by the father's toleration of so much illegitimacy, until he understands from Binard's swagger that he, Binard, has sired the three babies, and lives with his daughters all at once. The story ends up centring on Sido: Sido who was so jealously fond of Achille that she had looked ugly and disturbed when he had married.

> Sometimes she spoke violently about Monsieur Binard, calling him bitterly 'the corrupt widower', sometimes she let herself go off into commentaries...
> '... The child of the youngest one has eyelashes as long as *that*. I saw her the other day, she was suckling her baby on the doorstep, it was enchanting... After all... the ancient patriarchs...'
> But she suddenly became aware that I was only fifteen and a half and she went no further. (SC: 152–3)

Can we believe that Colette did not understand the implications of the stories she was writing? Sido must have felt sympathy for the man who had so well managed to do what she herself dreamt of doing: keep all her children under her roof, and satisfy them sexually. She symbolically effects this in 'L'Enlèvement' ('The Abduction'). Little Colette has heard tales of young girls being kidnapped, she is fascinated by an old-fashioned engraving on the staircase:

> It represented a post-chaise, harnessed to two queer horses

with necks like fabulous beasts'. In front of the gaping coach door a young man, dressed in taffeta, was carrying on one arm with the greatest of ease a fainting young woman. Her little mouth forming an 0, and the ruffled petticoats framing her charming legs, strove to express extreme terror. (*My M's H*: 42–3)

Sido herself is worried by the possibility of someone abducting her young. She has just lost Juliette through marriage. Little Colette has been moved away from her garret-room close to her mother's bedroom into Juliette's old room. One windy night, the door creaks. Two powerful arms lift her, wrapped in her sheets and blankets, rock her down the stairs. In a dream, she thinks she is being taken out of her mother's house:

> In such wise was I departing for the land where a post-chaise, amid the jangling of bells, stops before a church to deposit a young man dressed in taffeta and a young woman whose ruffled skirts suggest the rifled petals of a rose. I did not cry out. The arms were so gentle, so careful to hold me close enough to protect my dangling feet at every doorway. A familiar rhythm actually seemed to lull me to sleep in the abducting arms. (ibid.: 43)

It is Sido, of course, who like a mother-cat has, in the middle of the night, carried her little one back to her little room close to hers. Being kidnapped by her own mother is the perfection of bliss for the child. The arms that lift her combine strength and gentle protectiveness. They fulfil the desire for the mother which is in all children, girls and boys: which means, so Antoinette Fouque argues,[2] that all women are initially 'homo-sexual' in the sense that their first love-object is female like themselves. But in dream, and thanks to the engraving, Sido also fulfils the child's desire for elopement, for a man's strength and protective embrace, and the mysterious delights suggested by the rifled rose-petals. But the other desire that was to remain with Colette as with the other children, the desire to run back to the mother, the desire to be a child again, to have the mother within earshot after you have known sex, tried for adventure, that desire is also being fulfilled. For the little girl, waking up in a strange place that is none other than her old garret-room, can cry, to the one whose own cry had ever been, 'Where are the children?':

'Mother! Come quick! I've been abducted!'

Chapter Five

The Name of the Father II

> Their first name, their only name, one like the eye of the Cyclops.
>
> (Monique Wittig, *Les Guérillères*)

'The Abduction' throws a strange light on Colette's marriage to Willy. Everything that can be read about Willy's exploitation of his young wife, the fear which *My Apprenticeships* suggests she had of him, testimonies as to the power that he exerted over her, would lead you to think that Colette had married him because she was in awe of him, and that he was, for her, the powerful father that she never had. An experienced and sophisticated man, illumined by the prestige of fashionable Paris, almost old enough to be her father (fourteen years her senior), and looking it, Willy cut a figure. The Captain had lived in the aura of Sido.

Yet Willy the 'négrier', the driver of hacks, didn't have it in him any more than Captain Colette:

I have often thought that M. Willy suffered from a sort of agoraphobia, that he had a nervous horror of the blank page ... I fancy he was frequently overcome by fits of pathological shrinking, when he considered the courage, the grim fortitude that is needed to sit without disgust before the virgin field, the naked page, unscored by arabesques, headings, scratched-out words, the cold, indifferent paper, white and blinding, thankless, greedy. (*My Appr:* 70)

Willy collapsed into a state which Balzac (who knew what he was talking about, having spent his life-energies in struggle with the white paper) called by the old French term of 'déflocquement': 'the ghastly state of prostration that seems to turn the very bones to water, to unknit the fibres of the will' (*My Appr:* 71). Of course, it is Colette who is telling us, in the most devastatingly poised prose. And Colette it was who had previously written about the Captain's blank notebooks. But even if she exaggerated Willy's impotence, and was taking her revenge for the theft of her authorship at the time of the *Claudine* novels, she is still revealing something vital about her own relation to writing. Her father bequeathed her acres of blank space. Willy bid her fill exercise-books. 'I am called Claudine. I live in Montigny', are the first two sentences the young wife wrote. The name 'Claudine' mightily resembles the name 'Colette'. Montigny resembled Saint-Sauveur in everything but name. But Mont-igny suggests 'montagne', little mountain. Colline, Colette. The lady's first two sentences twice iterate the father's name.

Blank spaces, the licence to disguise, the order to tell. That was what Willy gave to Colette. His own incapacity became her power. Later, she was to draw parallels between her parents and Willy and herself. Her father had a wonderful collection of writing implements on his desk, she narrates in *Green Wax*. But he never wrote. Sido, on the other hand, could pen any number of sharp and elegant letters, sitting anyhow on a bale of hay, scribbling on any odd bit of paper. 'Our six daughters', Colette called the *Claudine* and *Minne* novels, as if Willy and herself, a couple like her own parents, had between the two of them engendered a spiritual offspring. She, easily writing in any odd corner; he, surrounded by all the attributes of the writer: but hardly writing a line.

To start with, Willy corrected the scripts, made suggestions, filled in bits of dialogue. He it was who (Brontë child-like) 'sprinkled' the *margins* with 'minute calculations, figures as wee as midges, as grains of sand' (*My Appr:* 21). He added a character called Henri Maugis (*mugis, maudis:* bellows, curses). A 'woman-fancier, all lit up with fatherly vice', fat Maugis loves 'puns and foreign drinks', is scholarly, fond of duelling, 'sentimental and unscrupulous' (*My Appr:* 57). He speaks like a compendium of Willy and the Usherette. He is Claudine's and even Minne's Ubu, appearing at every social gathering out of the depths of Poland, that is, Jarry would tell us, nowhere. He is Willy yielding to his own 'obsession for self-portraiture', as Claudine is Colette impersonating herself under a false name, being made to add 'a little spice to those childish affairs'. But as the writing went on, Colette also learnt to 'do' Maugis. When she wrote *Claudine and Annie*, Willy left an indication that he would fill in the gaps, and Colette handed him the complete script, saying, 'no gaps'. She could make the puppeteer's mirror-image into her own puppet.

And so, Colette ended up filling the margins too. She had gone a lot further with literacy than either of the two Cathys. Of course, there had been no Bible to start with. Only exercise-books. The only duty had been the imposition. No need to internalize the law. As long as the schoolmistress Melle Sergent or Master Willy were satisfied, rebel Claudine and her creator didn't have to care.

Yet, at that time, Colette's utmost ambition was to see herself figure on the title-page as Colette Willy.

Her first names were Sidonie-Gabrielle; she had been 'Gabri' for her family. Perhaps she began to hide the name when she went to Paris, to protect it. The habit for her to be called 'Colette' seems to have developed with her marriage.

Willy, a dazzling conversationalist and the protean member of clubs and cafés (such as the 'Cercle des Hydropathes' and the 'Chat noir') began early to assume a whole array of pen-names. As the drama critic of the review *Lutèce*, he signed as Henri Maugis (already), Jim Smiley and Boris Zichine, sometimes all three in the same number. He had become an author at a time when pseudonyms, switched genders and aliases of all kinds were in fashion. It was the period of late Symbolism, of decadence: and though Willy could never stomach so-called 'Decadents' like Erik Satie, you could say that a lot of the tricks of what we would loosely call 'decadence' got into his system.[1] Free verse had come into being in the 1880s, with Kahn and Laforgue. Poetic experiment-ation had been prodigious, and Mallarmé was still around. Indeed, Willy knew him. There was a spirit of cosmopolitanism abroad. Things English, American, Russian, were the cry. Among other things, Willy had translated Mark Twain. Pseudonyms played with all this. One of Willy's hacks called himself 'Curnonsky' – Latin: 'cur non?' (why not?), with a Russian-sounding ending: 'sky'. Willy at first substituted an English sounding 'y' for the 'i' of his first name: Henry for Henri. Then he remodelled the second barrel of his name (the 'Villars' of Gauthier-Villars), which was his grandmother's name: a 'w' and a 'y' were introduced, and there was 'Willy', full sexual joke intended.[2] Only, it was pronounced 'Vili' (though everyone in France now seems to say 'Willy'). It is interesting that the 'male' connotation of 'Willy' was based upon a female name (the grandmother's), not upon the patronymic. It all goes to show that Colette had a pretty explicit model to work on for her own name. It must be noted that Willy, like his gastronome of a friend, Curnonsky, had *one* name only. This custom was also adopted by some lady-writers of the period, like Rachilde. One of the best-known author of romances of the period, whom Henry James thought quite highly of, Gyp,[3] was, if you please, Sibylle Gabrielle Marie-Antoinette de Riqueti de Mirabeau, comtesse de Martel de Jouville. Willy, Gyp. A joke, a foreign joke. You pretend to be little, humble, when you know you're very BIG really. You use child-language, you invite the audience to a familiarity which socially would be unthinkable. Perhaps it was the popular end of the spectrum of the 'poetic revolution of language' Kristéva talks about.[4] It playfully debunked nationalism, the notion of a 'master language'. The literary and artistic salons which figure in *Claudine Married* as well as in *Un Amour de Swann* and *Du Côté des Guermantes* portray or parody the same world. The 1870 defeat was becoming forgotten, the Entente Cordiale was on the horizon, as was the Franco-Russian pact. Germany was Bayreuth, where Mme Verdurin takes Odette, just as Renaud takes Claudine, and they meet everybody else. Fashionable Europe was united in the worship of Wagner. There was nothing to inhibit all kinds of cross-border or cross-gender mutations in language.

Willy had married Colette partly out of gratitude to the Colette family for their kindness to his son Jacques.

Perhaps his early habit of calling young Gabrielle 'my pretty Colette' came from that. The name stuck.[5] Having been 'Willy' for so long, it must have seemed quite a conquest for her to be able to sign 'Colette Willy', which she did for *Creature Conversations*. She went on using that name for a long time, even after her separation from Willy in 1906. In part this may have been because she remained a long time attached to, fascinated by, Willy. Also, the name 'Willy' was fantastically well-known: thanks to the *Claudine* novels, yes, but people did not know who was the real author, and the name Willy would sell books, only God Almighty and Alfred Dreyfus were as famous, Sacha Guitry claimed.[6] The name 'Gabrielle Colette' would have had no impact at all. But, it also seems to me, choosing to be called Colette Willy, Colette was recognising the literariness of the writing persona she had decided to continue with.[7] This she did, even though she had officially exchanged her name for a very splendid one.

It is not unusual for a woman to fall in love for the second time with a man who has the same name as the first. After Henri Gauthier-Villars, there was Henry de Jouvenel des Ursins. The new Henry had a genuine, an aristocratic 'y', unlike the first, who had forged his out of anglomania. Colette's sensitivity to 'jambages', the legs or tails of letters that trail beneath the line and go wobbly when you are sick, may have been triggered by all these borrowed or genuine 'y's. A good way for a writer to learn to pay attention to every letter. The name of Henry de Jouvenel, at any rate, was hotly disputed. His first wife, Claire Boas, Bertrand's mother, held like grim death to the aristocratic canopy it put over her head. Colette was denied entry into an elegant hotel in Rome because she wanted to register as Baronne Henry de Jouvenel, and Baronne Henry de Jouvenel had just left. She had trouble proving her 'identity'. The competition for the man was hot indeed. Mme de Comminges, Renaud's mother and Jouvenel's mistress at the time when he met Colette and married her, pursued the couple with a loaded pistol throughout France and Switzerland. Either because the competition for the man took the form of a competition for his name, or because she was keen to become socially integrated, Colette became Madame Colette de Jouvenel in town. But not Gabrielle de Jouvenel. And as an author she remained Colette Willy.

But she was also complicating the pattern in a way that is reminiscent of her family's way of proceeding, no longer of Willy's. She called her daughter, her only child, as Achille had called one of his, her god-daughter: Colette. Thus there were two Colette de Jouvenel, the mother, the daughter. Sido had had two identical little girls, her father's daughter, and Gabri. She had also called Gabri like herself: *Sidonie*-Gabrielle. Catherine Earnshaw, etc.... Perhaps Colette meant to keep alive the family all of whose members but one were now dead: the Captain had died in 1905, Juliette in 1907 (suicide), Sido in 1912, Achille a year later. Only Léo, the tender musician was left, and he had no children, was not even married. It was left to the daughter's daughter to carry on the patronymic. But also, the name 'Colette', in the mother's correspondence, seems to mean 'chéri', darling. She wields it like a term of love, making it descend in turns upon her husband or granddaughter, allowing identity to mutate inside the 'nom propre'. It becomes a tribal name, there to designate the object of affection.

The marriage to Jouvenel collapsed in 1923, the year in which the single name 'Colette' figured on the title-page of *The Ripening Seed*. Colette started living with Maurice Goudeket in 1925. But she never took his name. She remained Colette, on the title-page of her books. Madame Colette, in town, as her mother had been. She becomes her father and her mother.

Colette reaches her full identity as a writer when she's rid herself of all names except her father's. Writing, she fills the blank notebooks dedicated lovingly to Sido. She wins the love of her mother. She becomes the several people the mother called Colette.

Colette: the father, but also the name spoken by the mother, and made plural by means of her speech.

Part II
Towards the Centre of the Rose

Chapter Six

Figures of Love and Desire

'Was Will das Weibe?', 'What does woman want?', is the question Freud asked, and could not answer. Twentieth-century psychoanalysis and literature have produced reams of paper in attempts to answer it. Lacan has claimed that women themselves cannot say. Femininity is a mystery, feminine desire has been made into the holy of holies. The 'dark continent', as Freud called it, a pre-civilization lying far beneath civilization such as we know it, the Oedipus complex, as the pre-Minoan lies beneath the civilization of Greece.

One simple answer, one that has been sounded from George Sand's *Lélia* to Colette's own *Duo*, is that women aren't that special: they shouldn't be made to carry such abysses nor such heights.[1] Female desire is only a mystery for men, who want it to play this or that role in their complicated constructs. Perhaps one should say simply, women want the same things as men. They want everything. They want happiness. Perhaps they want God. What life is about, the indispensable. But perhaps they don't want it in the same way. Their route is more direct. They often call it love. When men hear what they say, they reply, 'But that cannot possibly be it. Where is the mystery, the darkness, the Sturm-und-Drang, the Revelation? You do not speak your *real* desire, because this is what you cannot say.' And so it goes.

I cannot escape the thought that good Dr Freud might not have found the mystery of female desire quite so impenetrable if, in the years in which he first conceived it, he had bothered to read young Madame Willy. Of course, he could not know that it was Madame, not Monsieur, who was then writing. And it wouldn't have solved his problem, for the mystery of femininity he was envisaging was in himself, and he needed to project it.

It would be a fascinating exercise to work out in detail how Colette is a counterpoint to Freud, though she was no more aware of him than he was of her. For most, perhaps all, of Colette's work is about desire, the gradual creation of identity through projection in language. It is a painful, changeable, infinitely complex series of projections, a search for fulfilment of the desire to *relate*: to 'the world of sense', food, forests, flora, fauna, other women, children, adolescents, men, relatives and friends. To relate irreverently, greedily, tremblingly, graspingly, respectfully. To relate in and through love, in a total dedication of self, to what is to her totally and continuously engrossing. Her prose gives itself, it pays absorbed, cunning, wicked, startled attention to its infinitely changing objects. In no other work perhaps is there such a complete awareness of the reality principle. In no other work, a greater readiness to give oneself to the object of desire, such growing knowledge that successful relations in language require the same resources as relations in love. In no other work, therefore, is there greater *sanity*. Colette is your twentieth-century recipe against neurosis. Colette, the anti-Dora, the counter-poison.

The maternal uncle

For interestingly, it was in 1900, the year of *Claudine At School*, that Freud treated Dora. The case is so well-known, and so much discussion of it is now available,[2] that I shall only offer the briefest reminder. Eighteen-year-old 'Dora' (Freud's disguise name for Ida Bauer) had been brought to Freud by her father, who knew him quite well socially. Dora was suffering from hysterical symptoms – migraine, dyspnoea, coughing, even occasional loss of her voice. As Dora's story unfolded – if that's the right word for something requiring so much interpretation, got at in fits and starts, dialogue and dreams – it turned out that her symptoms dated from the complex involvement of her family with the K's. Dora's father got on badly with her mother (who suffered from a cleanliness mania, housewife's psychosis), and had been engaged for some years in an affair with a young and beautiful woman, Frau K. At the same time, as a cover-up and perhaps compensation, Dora had been pushed by her father into the company of Herr K. She was also fond of the K. children, whom she looked after; fond also, and on an intimate footing with, Frau K., who educated her, lent her books. Dora's first loss of voice dated from her being kissed by Herr K. in his office when she was fourteen. The symptoms had been renewed after he had, when she was sixteen, propositioned her by a lake: she had slapped his face, but her family's, especially her father's, readiness to disbelieve her account of this and believe instead Herr K.'s assurances, backed by Frau K., that she had made up the whole story, had brought about an aggravation of the hysterical symptoms. The world of adults had, in effect, conspired to deny the adolescent girl access to the reality principle. Her father, though Freud in some ways sees him, and Herr K. (a substitute father-figure), as the object of Dora's unconscious desire, had failed to act as protector of his daughter's inviolacy.

If 'The Abduction', with all its graceful air of anecdote, does, as I have argued, articulate something important about the complexity and contradictory nature of a young girl's dream of bliss, it is easy to see how dreadfully deprived and perverted Dora was. She was denied her dream of a romantic seducer: her father acted as her surreptitious pander, he exchanged her with Herr K. for Frau K. She had no elbow-room for desire, for elopement. And she was also denied a maternal/paternal refuge after the elopement. No crying, 'Mummy, come quick! I've been abducted' for poor Dora. Her mother offered no protection; all she presented her with was her own damaged and compulsively cleaning ego. And her father, instead of being her protector, her home guardian, was a dishonest accomplice in her corruption. But he also acted the patriarch, at one with Herr K. and, he hoped, Freud, against the denunciation by the young girl. Dora was being both subjected to the patriarchal exchange of women, and made to take part in an incestuous network.

Yet if what happened to Dora is practically the reverse of what happened to Colette, there are a number of respects in which the 'Claudine' case and the Dora case are similar. Dora it was who revealed her story to patriarchal Freud; Freud it was who wrote it, authored it. Colette it was who, supposedly, told her story to Willy, while Willy supposedly wrote it as the *Claudine* novels, and actually authored it. Freud wrote the Dora case straight after the girl had interrupted the treatment, had left him, in 1900; but afterwards he could not get the date straight, and though the manuscript had been accepted by a review, he did not send it, but kept it for four years in a *drawer* – rather the way M. Willy had kept the exercise-books of *Claudine At School* in the drawer of his desk. Surprising what deep drawers they had, those apparently so patriarchal men. Surprising also how their 'sources', and 'real-life' characters fought them over authorship. Colette filled in all the gaps; she ended up having Claudine first leave Renaud, at the end of *Claudine Married* – temporarily. But then Annie left her husband for good in *Claudine and Annie*, Colette left Willy, however unwillingly, and Claudine left the series for good: *Claudine s'en va*. Dora struggled with Freud over every bit of interpretation. She ended up having the whole thing out with her family and with the K's. And leaving Freud himself, with his unfinished account, his unperplexed puzzles and projections. Ida Bauer herself never got rid of Dora: how could she, there had been too much damage, and no real help? But she had made a brave attempt. Colette did fight clear of Claudine. It took her twenty years. But then, her father had not been a pander, and her mother never wavered in her protective love.

It is perhaps highly revealing of *fin-de-siècle* mores that, neither in the Dora case nor in the five *Claudine* novels is there more than the shadow of a young man. Young girls seem to be given over to, destined almost for, older men. I do not know whether anyone has applied Malinowski's findings[3] to the marriage patterns of the period.* But in fiction as in middle- and upper-class

---

*I'm not suggesting that the maternal uncle in Malinowski is a comparable figure – in fact, he is almost the reverse, and it is the paternal aunt who is the lawful, and even sexually recommended relation. But the whole pattern and variations of the kinship taboos as described by Malinowski could have fascinating applications.

families, the figure of what could be called the 'maternal uncle' holds sway.[4] Either a middle-aged man who has a connection with the mother, or the mother's actual younger brother, marries the girl. One may well wonder why. Was the social circle so limited, that the uncle was one of the few eligible bachelors? Were there questions of dowry at stake? Or was the custom of the man getting married so much later, after he'd got a livelihood, established himself, sown his wild oats, so widespread that it led to this? That certainly is a frequent marriage pattern in Balzac's *La Comédie humaine*. Félix de Vandenesse, the hero of *Le Lys dans la vallée*, waits till he is well into his thirties and has drained the cup of love before, in *Une Fille d'Eve*, marrying a young virgin. Colette's marriage to Willy was of this kind. And Dora's circle seems to find it perfectly natural that she should have advances made by a man old enough to be her father. Is it that, in a period of artistic revolution, that type of coupling, which savoured of incest, was a modest way of defying a taboo – or, on the contrary, does it reveal a society given over to the pursuit of incest? At any rate, in fiction as in life, the figure of the maternal uncle is deeply attractive (like the boss to the secretary, the doctor to the nurse, in today's Mills and Boons). There is *Mon Oncle et mon curé*, Gyp's *Le Mariage de Chiffon* in popular fiction – and *Claudine in Paris*. 'My cousin the uncle', as Claudine calls Renaud, may have silver in his hair and tiny wrinkles on his temples. The 'little girl' still gets drunk on the 'eyes that turn black in the evening lights' as much as on *Asti*, and she goes limp like 'asphalt that is still warm' on the uncle's shoulder. It's not just that an adolescent, tipsy, precociously knowing, market-geared relish for man makes her 'overflow like a vase' and tell Renaud of the green, absinth-scented pieces of rock she used to lick to a sharp tip at school. Mixed with the 'nymphette' confessions is the knowledge that, because of her absentee, moon-crazed father, she needs a 'daddy, a friend, a lover' all rolled into one. 'No place is sweet to me, except his shoulder where, nestling, my lips almost touched his neck... Oh Claudine,Claudine, how you become a child again as you feel yourself becoming a woman!' (*C At S*: 362–3).

What Claudine wants is what many seem to want. Nanda is in love with her mother's 'friend' (lover?) Vanderbank in James's *The Awkward Age* (1899). In *What Maisie Knew* (1897) Maisie makes a bid for Sir Claude, her mother's ex-second husband and her stepmother's lover: a doubly maternal uncle, Sir Claude, fair, soft, charming, gallant, is very similar to Renaud (though more of a child and as such, probably nicer).They combine maturity, the prestige of makeshift fatherliness, seductiveness, and something feminine. The avuncular seducer is fair, and his moustache sweetly smells of blond tabacco... But it is only in the romances that he fulfils the maiden's dreams. Nanda and Maisie fail to get their man. Claudine is initiated to much sexual pleasure by Renaud's expert caresses, but, in *Claudine Married*, she remains strangely dissatisfied, enervated, perhaps, she puts it to herself, because she wanted a master she could fear a little. Minne, in *L'Ingénue libertine*, is for a long time disappointed in her husband, an older cousin on her mother's side, much too safe for her taste. Only Gigi, the heroine of a novel written by Colette almost fifty years later but made to take place in the period of the *Claudine* novels, will have a fairy-tale fate. 'Tonton', 'nuncle', the mature millionaire and friend of the ladies of the family, turns out to be in love with her as she is in love with him. She's been brought up to become a courtesan, but 'Tonton' is so much in love he makes an honest woman of her. And so, like little Aggie in *The Awkward Age*, Gigi gets the millionaire she's been brought up to entrap: unlike Aggie, she loves her millionaire. Fresh, long-limbed as a young colt, and beautifully undamaged by all the pandering around her, Gigi also exorcizes the shade of Claudine.

Freud's Dora belongs with that group of heroines. Her situation is not unlike Maisie's. Herr K., who propositions her, is the husband of her father's mistress (as Sir Claude is the lover of Maisie's father's wife – if you follow me). Like Colette, who looked after little Jacques Gauthier-Villars (Willy's son) prior to marrying Willy, Dora plays with the K. children. Also, she strangely seems drawn to Frau K. herself . . .

Caught inside an incestuous set-up, her mother reduced to 'nothing' ('my wife is nothing to me,' Dora's father tells Freud), betrayed by her father and by Frau K., Dora becomes hysterical. She loses her voice. Colette instead gradually learnt to fill the blanks. But she had known depression, she had known despair. One year after her marriage to Willy, she nearly died of pining.

I have spoken of the 'maternal uncle' rather than of a 'father figure' or simply uncle not only because the mature seducer is often the mother's brother or someone who associates with the mother, or the women in the family, but because his attraction to the young girl is of a deeply ambiguous, *androgynous* kind. Would it be preposterous to suggest that in Renaud Claudine seeks, not only a substitute daddy, but a love akin to that of her defunct and unmentioned mother? And that, marrying Willy, Colette herself had married both her father and her mother, had found in one man, the social equivalent of Herr K., something like Dora's father and Frau K. rolled into one? Or thought she had . . . You can speak of Willy's flamboyant maleness: he fights duels, has lots of affairs: his regular mistresses call him 'papa', the passing

ones, 'uncle'. He runs sweat-shops, is a great editor. Yet there was a feminine side to the man. Either that, or Colette constructed one when she wrote *My Apprentice-ships*. Obviously, the 'real' Willy I'm talking about is the Willy of Colette's carefully engineered autobiographies. She hints at his soft rotundity, his 'bullfinch' paunch.*
Caricaturists who portrayed him as a brothel Madame, displaying his prize girls, Colette and Polaire, were perhaps not widely off the mark. Willy did play with female *alter egos*, he signed his musical reviews 'the Usherette', he nicknamed himself 'Doucette', 'softie'. Colette, Doucette. Echoing diminutives, both feminine. In *Creature Conversations*, Toby-Chien, the he-dog, deter-mined, faithful, simple, is Claudine's dog. Kiki-la-Doucette, the she-cat, cunning, nonchalant, queenly, loves Renaud, and seems a revelation of his secret character. Kiki-la-Doucette is also like an 'apache' name, a name for one of the subtle 'mauvais garçons', the adolescent gang-leaders whom Minne dreams of. You'd think it had come out of Genêt, or rather, antedated Genêt. Kiki, Willy, 'Vili'. Kiki, Doucette, Kékette, quéquette. 'Quéquette' is the childish French name for penis, the equivalent to 'willy'. Willy's cat-name puns with the very combination of virile strength and soft tenderness which pertain to the mother, in 'The Abduction'. In this, he must have appeared to Colette to be able to fulfil a desire she felt, but did not know she had. By the time she wrote 'The Abduction' she knew. But that was thirty years later.

It does look indeed as if, in that whole period of her marriage to Willy, Colette showed signs of a complex and puzzled androgyny, both in terms of her desires and

---

*Is there a suggestion of pregnancy in that belly? In that case, which is the father, which the mother, of the 'six daughters', the *Claudine* and the *Minne*?

of the persona that could strike out for the fulfilment of those desires. It is useful, here again, to recall that Dora (Freud understood at the end of the case-study, relegating the insight to a footnote) felt a strong love for Frau K. Frau K. was several figures rolled into one for Dora: initiator (she lent her books about sex), mentor (she encouraged her to study), substitute-mother (she was beautiful, tender, charming, her father's mistress and as such a kind of stepmother). She was also the object of her desire, and in this, Dora was her father's *rival*. Dora never seemed to get to the state when she could formulate and act out her homosexual desires. In this, Colette differed vastly from her.

The second

Not long after her move to Paris as a young bride, Colette received an anonymous letter. She went to the address she was given, where she found Willy with a dark young woman called Charlotte Kinceler. Charlotte got hold of a pair of long scissors, and who knows what might have happened, Colette suggests, if she had not said something neutral. It was a major moment of choice, and has its place for good reasons in *My Apprenticeships*. The decision *not* to regard the other woman as the enemy will have many consequences. No doubt waves of bitter rivalry ebbed and flowed between the two women. Colette was to suffer deeply from jealousy, and she often wrote about it. But neither pouncing on Charlotte, nor letting Charlotte pounce on her, she was doing more than being cowardly, or sensible, or compliant. For she went on to become Charlotte's friend, and throughout her life would build major friendships with other women: Marguerite

Moréno, Annie de Pène, Germaine Beaumont, Claude Chauvière, Renée Hamon, many more. In her fiction too, relations between women will play a major role: complicity, in enmity as in love, will be there early. And with it, forms of understanding that run almost beneath the text, a peculiar elusiveness in the exchanges between characters, in the ways in which the text allows objects to be glimpsed, not seen, and yet remembered. A world comes into being in which either/or does not function, because traditional forms of couplings and confrontation did not become established for Colette. In that moment when Charlotte was poised with the scissors, Colette stretched a hand towards her, related towards the other point of the (deadly) eternal triangle. And thus became released from the head, angle A.

In *La Seconde* (*The Other One*, which is a mistranslation), the relation between the two women, Fanny and Jane, who are in love with the same man, Farou, is of such importance and complexity in its own right that when their rivalry has been declared and they're having it out, they ask Farou to leave the room: so they can concentrate on working out something that is in excess of their relationship with *him*. C's relation to B is as important as C's relation to A, or B to A... There is an actual *equality* in the world of relationships Colette created that Simone de Beauvoir never suspected. But then, Simone de Beauvoir always was an either/or type of person. It is ironic that she should have thought of that title, *La Seconde*, for what was to be named, after a man's suggestion, *Le Deuxième sexe*. 'The Second Sex', as a title, implies that one sex is first. It implies the Hegelian master/slave relationship. Or it implies lack, scarcity. Only one can have, be a full-size human being. The other is... the Other. (Which is why the title, *The Other One*, is so inappropriate.) Nothing is further from Colette than the notion that the female sex should be second in anything. *La Seconde* is the second woman in Farou's life, the second person in Fanny's life, the woman who secunds (helps) Fanny and Farou and buoys them up, the second during which Fanny perceives what is going on between Farou and Jane. Of Farou, Colette wrote that he was one of her few successful male characters because he was so strongly borne up by the two women characters who are involved with him. You run round the points of a triangle in which nobody is the head. Or else, the angle has been opened so wide that it reaches 180 degrees. You run up and down it, like fingers on piano keys, and angles can start from any of its points.

Androgyny, and homosexualitites

Willy had sensed best-seller material in Colette's school memories because they were first-hand accounts of a range of experience your average (male) author found it most difficult to come by: adolescent secrets. Males did not enter girls' schools, except as Inspectors. City people, a middle-class readership, knew nothing about primary education in the country. But Willy also insisted that 'some spice' be added to 'those childish affairs'. He knew that, even more than stories about adolescent peasants, his readers would want lesbian choice morsels. Lolitas were probably in shorter supply then than they are now. Fresh-baked tales about their dalliance with each other would sell like hot cakes. They did. So good was the vein Willy found he had tapped with *Claudine At School* that he repeated the operation twice. He made Meg Villars, his second wife, write the supposedly English boarding-school book *Les Imprudences de Peggy*. And his third, Swiss wife, Madeleine de Swarte, produced *Mady écolière*. You've got to give it to the man: he knew a fruitful transaction when he saw one! The trick was to recognize Meg in Peggy, and Madeleine in Mady. Serial daughters, Dresden china made in Japan, then Hong Kong...

The vein was indeed a rich one. For complicated reasons[5] there had been, in nineteenth-century art and literature, some licence to *represent* lesbianism; whereas the taboo on the representation of male homosexuality was much stronger. For instance, Balzac's *La Fille aux yeux d'or* actually introduces the reader into the white and gold bedroom of the two women lovers, Paquita and Mariquita – even though the actual love-making that takes place is that of the hero, De Marsay, and Paquita... But Balzac never enters the bedroom of Vautrin and Lucien de Rubempré, the homosexual couple of *Splendeurs et misères des courtisanes*. One strong reason for the artistic licence regarding lesbians might be that representing them disturbs nothing, it falls into a patriarchal pattern. The (male) author[6] indulges in a controlling, sophisticated kind of voyeurism: he can penetrate the intimacy of women's bodies, be where in life he is not, gain access to a holy of holies. And it also enables him to relate indirectly to his own homosexuality. Thus Verlaine boasts that he is 'l'égal de la grande Sappho' in his multiple love-making. Théophile Gautier, the most honest of them all, admits to the doubleness of his desires in *Mademoiselle de Maupin*. Baudelaire wanted to call *Les Fleurs du mal*, *Les Lesbiennes*, Courbet paints lesbians asleep in each other's arms; the sonnet 'Une négresse' enables Mallarmé to display the tender, affrighted, titillating young flesh of a young girl laid by an animal-like and demon-tossed negress... What high art won't do! Mallarmé's faun pursues and seizes two nymphs, also in each other's arms. They elude him, and his frustrated yearning swells his pipe with song. His reed is a 'twin' reed. He *needed* two...

So did Willy. But he let no one escape him. A recent biographer has described how, when as a young student he went to brothels, he favoured 'doing it' with two very young girls. He even got it free, sometimes, when his triangular frolics gave pleasure to an ageing voyeur. Part of Colette's appeal for him was that she was a nymph, with the potential of nymphs to offer twinned forms to the faun that he felt himself to be.

Willy's are an extreme example of the attitudes and circumstances that allowed Paris to become 'the mecca of lesbianism in the late nineteenth century'.[7] Perhaps because, as Catherine Van Casselaer argues, the revolutionary tradition of liberty was still alive in France, or because the Code Napoléon ignored lesbianism, or again because there was no single group or institution that was 'self-confident enough to pre-empt the role of arbiter of social and therefore sexual mores', Paris in that period had become 'the undisputed pleasure-capital of the world, the place where inhibitions could be shed'. Provincial and foreign lesbians flocked to the 'second Gomorrah'. Transvestism, actual and imaginary, gradually gained currency. It had been exceptional at first. The painter Rosa Bonheur (who died in 1899) had been allowed to dress as a man by special 'permission de transvestissement' of the Prefect of Police so she could go to the slaughter-houses and the very down-to-earth Marché aux Chevaux in Paris (so she could paint them), and Mme Jane Dieulafoy who had fought alongside her husband in the Franco-Prussian war continued after 1870 to wear men's clothes, using as an excuse her need to accompany her husband in his archaeological expeditions – she was later to become a well-known society hostess and literary figure. Rachilde, who started her career as a journalist with one of the first feminist magazines, *L'Ecole des femmes*, and went on to become famous with her 'patently infamous book', *Monsieur Vénus* (which Oscar Wilde was accused to have read during his trial), a 'blend of hermaphroditism, homosexuality, prostitution and transvestism',[8] also had a 'permission de transvestissement'. She held a powerful position when Colette entered the lists as source/author of the *Claudine* and became her friend, admirer and protector. But from the turn of the century onwards no further 'permission de transvestissement' seemed to be needed, despite the efforts of the then Prefect of Police, Lépine. The actress Sarah Bernhardt and her lover Louise Abbéma had long dressed in various masculine guises. The floodgates opened. The group that rotated round the flamboyant Natalie Clifford-Barney (an American whom Colette portrayed as Flossie in *Claudine Married*), and that which hung around Colette's lesbian lover of later years, Missy, and Colette herself at times in those years, all dressed as men. Lesbian affairs often occupied the centre of the stage. Natalie openly pursued beautiful Liane de Pougy, then English poetess Renée Vivien, a touching figure, over-influenced, according to Colette (whose version Natalie contested) by decadent models and Baudelairian images of lesbians. Eva Palmer, Romaine Brooks, Lucie Delarue-Mardrus, all literary figures, pursued their often long-lasting relationships in broad daylight. Natalie's erotic 'tableaux vivants' and her public though select entertainments in her pavillon in the rue Jacob, in which Mata-Hari rode in naked on a white horse, were confidently performed. Poetess Anna de Noailles was more discreet, but the charismatic, pathetically ugly, pacifist Rémy de Gourmont, one of the high priests of Symbolism and a remarkable critic, made no bones about his infatuation with famous lesbians like Moulin Rouge Jane Avril, whom Lautrec painted, and later Natalie herself. Missy and Colette appeared in public in a variety of places, the most noticed of course being the Moulin Rouge stage for the scandalous *Rêve d'Egypte*.

Thus the context in which *Claudine At School* appeared was favourable from the point of view of the representation of adolescent lesbians. There was the commercial, the voyeuristic appeal, yes. There was also genuine interest, and when people like Rachilde championed Colette, they must have recognized that there was something fresh, convincing, fun and, as Catherine Van Casselaer argues, uniquely 'neutral'[9] in the period in Colette's depiction of the friendships, rivalries and intimacies of the girls in Saint-Sauveur. When Colette wrote it, and even when she rewrote it, urged by Willy to add 'some spice' to those 'childish affairs' she was not really acquainted with the world of lesbian Paris. That came later, in the wake of the success of the book and the following *Claudine*. She seems to have added Melle Aimée, the pretty sub-mistress whom Claudine desires but loses to the headmistress, Melle Sergent, as an afterthought, at Willy's prompting: she is one of the few characters in *Claudine At School* that biographers have been unable to trace back to a 'real life person' in Saint-Sauveur.

Yet, whatever Willy's influence, it was Colette who did write – it seems (the manuscript has been lost, so Willy's 'additions' cannot be verified). Willy *licenced* Colette in relation to homosexual desire, in an age in which men insisted on ownership of their wives and on their wives' virtue if no one else's. Of course, it's a limited kind of licence, only extending, as Renaud makes clear in *Claudine Married*, to women:

'You women can do anything. It's charming and it's of no consequence whatever.... It's the logical search for a more perfect partner, for a beauty more like your own, which reflects your own sensitiveness and your own weaknesses.... If I dared (but I shouldn't dare), I would say that certain women need women in order to preserve their taste for men.' (*CM*: 99)

But whatever the control and long-range profit that there is in Renaud's, as in Willy's toleration of his wife's lesbian affairs, Colette the writer was given the elbow-room to explore the range of her desires, and to search for herself in the process. She was a *country*-girl, blissfully unaware of Parisian images of 'Decadence'. It is also certainly significant that, in her love for Melle Aimée, Claudine, who is fifteen, when Melle Aimée is in her early twenties, possibly a 'mother' type of figure, is the seducer, active in her pursuit, cunning in her machinations to get Melle Aimée. It is equally significant that rivalry for Melle Aimée, 'Beloved', the arch-female, too pliant, easily frightened, should be with Melle Sergent, whose military-style virility brings out Claudine's own. Claudine leads the camp of the pupils, Melle Sergent attempts to quell the sedition. Claudine is also very much the 'Mac', the toughie, with Luce, Melle Aimée's young sister, in love with Claudine and cravenly hanging on to her. Claudine bullies Luce, roughs her up, boxes her ears, and generally fends off her advances very much in the way in which, years later, the protagonist of *The Shackle* to whom 'feminine' Renée loses her heart, Jean, beats his mistress May. There is a long road to travel before Colette's 'heroine' has mutated from Claudine into Renée. Or should I say, before part of Claudine has gone over to Jean?

However much, in those turn of the century years, Colette may have written at Willy's prompting and to make money, and however unsavoury the reader, may find some of the titillating moments in the *Claudine* and in the *Minne* novels, as she herself did retrospectively, there still is, in the production of that whole period, a moving quest for what the heart desires, and the impressive ability to go for it. Claudine and Minne find out what they want by doing it. And it isn't what they want, so they do the next thing. Androgynous Claudine, freshly recovered from a grave illness, indulges in voyeuristic confessions with homosexual Marcel, her cousin who looks like a girl, as she herself, with her newly cropped hair, looks like a boy. Marcel gets high on descriptions of goings-on between nubile girls. Is this a parody of the readership? (If the cap fits, reader, wear it: if you get excited by the same things as Marcel, well, you know who you are.) Or a foray into hermaphroditism of the kind that Rachilde's *Monsieur Vénus* perhaps had made possible? Or is ailing Claudine, who has never been with a man, being gently led into men, made to go through all the stages of the spectrum, from Melle Aimée to Luce to Marcel to Renaud, the maternal uncle? But then even the relative heterosexuality that Renaud offers does not appease Claudine. '*En ménage*', an ironic title if ever there was one, she falls in love, for the first time ever perhaps, with Rézi.

That is an extraordinarily ambiguous and interesting affair. There is a sense in which Rézi is to Claudine what Frau K. was to Dora. A beautiful woman, her father/fatherly husband's friend, a bit older than herself, more of a woman of the world: but above all, excitingly *feminine*. Ah, what a word to use, when I am in the midst of the spectrum! Hélène Cixous says of Dora that she is *her father's daughter*. That means, among other things, that Dora has the qualities of decisiveness and initiative that characterize her father. Also, she is her father's rival, as

Claudine is Melle Sergent's rival, and, as it turns out, as she is Renaud's rival for the love of Rézi. Yet in *Claudine Married* the effect of Claudine falling more and more deeply under the spell of Rézi is to feminize her, soften and bewilder the tomboy in her. Rézi is introduced as all curves and spirals, she is lace and flounces and undress and scents, and the intoxication that this produces in Claudine brings out the woman in her. It is Rézi who seduces her. Claudine however is also the dominant partner sexually, acting the part of the injured husband at the end when she finds that Rézi has betrayed her with her own husband Renaud. Her passion of fury is directed at Rézi, not Renaud. And yet the relationship between the two women is fascinatingly poised in terms of gender. Colette was to write 'The Abduction' years later but there is a draft of it in *Claudine Married*, an imaginative abduction in the course of which Claudine is in turns bride and bridegroom:

> 'Rézi, don't talk to me any more. I'm in a trance of laziness and well-being. Don't force me to get up from here.... Imagine that it's night and we're travelling.... Imagine the wind in your hair ... bend down, that low branch might wet your forehead!... Squeeze close against me – mind out, the water in the deep ruts is splashing up under the wheels....'
> All her supple body followed my game with a treacherous compliance. Her hair, tossed back from the head that lay on my shoulder, brushed against my face like the twigs I had invented to distract me from inner turmoil.

> 'I'm travelling,' she murmured.
> 'But shall we arrive?'
> Her two hands nervously gripped my free one.
> 'Yes, Claudine. We shall arrive.'
> 'Where?'
> 'Bend down, and I'll whisper to you.'

Credulously, I obeyed. And it was her mouth that I
encountered. I listened for a long time to what her mouth
told mine.... She had not lied; we were arriving....
(*CM*: 120–121)

Claudine is acting the part given to Sido in 'The
Abduction', but her 'trance of laziness', her listening to
what Rézi's voice is telling her, are also the bride's part.
But though it will be Sido who in the later piece will
fulfil the dream of a bridegroom, there is little of
'primary' homosexuality, it seems to me, in the
relationship between Claudine and Rézi. There is little
of the mother in Rézi, though she is older and more
confident than Claudine. Claudine's seduction of her
does not seem to me to be seduction of the mother, nor
seduction by the mother, but almost a case of narcissism.
It is almost as if Claudine learned to love her own
muffled or suppressed femininity by loving Rézi. Thus
for instance cropped Claudine brushes Rézi's hair:

> prolonged contact with this golden stuff that I unravel and
> that is so electric that it clings to my dress and crackles
> under the tortoiseshell comb, like burning bracken, is too
> much for me. The magic of that intoxicating hair penetrates
> all through me and makes me torpid.... Weakly, I let fall the
> loosened sheaf and Rézi becomes impatient – or pretends
> to. (*CM*: 120–1)

This is perhaps the place to warn the English reader
who might not suspect this how much is lost by
translation. I do not have the space to show this at
length, but as I have already mentioned how much
Colette cares about relations between words, and will
later go on to talk about her excitement about accuracy,
the point is worth making. In the original, 'this golden
stuff that I unravel...' is 'cette étoffe d'or que j'effiloche,

qui . . . crépite sous le râteau d'écaille comme une fougère qui s'embrase'. It is a gold *cloth*, fabric, that is being *frayed* by the comb: the comb itself is not named, 'râteau' is a rake, and its raking gradually *ignites* the bracken. There is also the sound, of course: '. . . qui s'attache, électrique, à ma robe et crépite sous le râteau de'écaille comme une fougère qui s'embrase'. You hear the crackling of the hair, you are being intoxicated by the sound.

I insist, because all this is quite vital, and so much is lost even in the good translations. It's not just that Colette creates Claudine's intoxication through the precision of her naming and image making ('s'effiloche', which comes from 'fil', thread, and has a home-spun flavour, is wonderfully suggestive). It is also that she is recuperating and altering worlds of representation of females, especially in the later part of the nineteenth-century. Hair, for instance, has a loaded history: there is Baudelaire's 'La Chevelure', followed by countless others, including, when Colette is writing the *Claudine* novels, Pierre Louÿs's 'La Chevelure' and Mélisande's hair . . . Not to mention Symbolist and 'Decadent' representations of women's hair, Whistler's 'Girl in White', Moreau's 'Salomes', Rosetti and Beardsley and whole pictures of female hair entrapping men, men's faces, in Munch and Toorop and Klimt.* There is Maupassant's story about a young officer who finds himself in a haunted bedroom, confronted by a girl with mane-like long black hair, who holds out a comb to him and says, 'Please comb my hair'. She disappears, but when he finds himself in the courtyard and is told that no one lives in the castle, he finds a long thick hair wound round one of the buttons of his tunic . . . Madame

---

*I have in mind in particular Toorop's *The Three Brides* (1893) where the stylized hair winds itself around everything.

Bovary's hair, 'électrique', gets caught on the rough cloth of Rodolphe's riding-jacket. 'O toison, moutonnant jusque sur l'encolure!' The woman's hair, fleece-like, shows her to be all animal, and all sex. It manifests her power, dangerous and entrancing as that of nature, to engulf man. In the Pierre Louÿs or the Maeterlinck, it is a wonderful, atavistic power. In nearly everybody else, it is terrifying, a sign of woman's dual nature, sphinx-like, destructive. The woman-with-the-long-hair lures, then decapitates, castrates.

> 'Je plongerai ma tête amoureuse d'ivresse
> Dans ce noir océan où l'autre est enfermé...'

Claudine is moved by the same impulse: 'la magie de ces cheveux enivrants me pénètre et m'engourdit...' but the – oh dear, what is the right word? – earthiness of her images means that the hair is given back to itself as hair. There is knowledge about the experience of combing, and communication of that experience in the 's'effiloche'. And the rake crackling in the bracken makes a sound and a visual image that both bring out the actual colour of the hair (red, tawny, luminous) but also make you picture a stretch of bracken catching fire, take pleasure in the illusion of knowledge that is being given to you. Together with a sense of magic, there is a sense of actuality, of delight in this world. So that Rézi as woman is not forgotten, whereas the immense appeal of Baudelaire's poem (whose magnificence is not in doubt) depends upon the disappearance of the mistress as a person. Colette, on the other hand, trading in the images of her predecessors and contemporaries, is reclaiming their actuality. In the process she is imaginatively reclaiming her own body: wasn't her own hair, so recently cut, similar to Rézi's, and isn't her knowledge of its sound and colour based on what you could call twenty-odd years of the experience of living with it? 'My masterpiece', Sido called that hair: 'and you've cut it', she reproached Colette. Perhaps the women in that period had to cut it, as they all did, Natalie Clifford-Barney and Eva Palmer and Lucie Delarue-Mardrus, because the weight of the men's images had become too heavy to carry? 'You tell me it is like a fleece, a forest, the ocean, the sky, a rope: that I am an animal, nature itself. Look, I've cut it, it's short like yours: I am a human being.' Pity, all the same, that they did have to cut it.

So keen was Willy to get fictional and monetary revenues from his wife's erotic speculations that he gave her free rein the way few other married women at the time must have had it. A true Bohemian, he effaced the distinction between wife and prostitute. All he insisted upon was the dividends. He thus allowed Colette to go to an all-women soirée at Natalie Clifford-Barney's on condition that... presumably, that she tell him all, or make use of it for his benefit. But doing so, he had created for Colette the opportunity to have relations of an intimate kind. All she would have to do would be to cut the chain that, she told Natalie who narrates this episode, she was ashamed Natalie had seen. And there she would be.

Cut the chain is almost what Claudine does, at the end of *Claudine Married*. She runs away, back to her native village, after she's found what dividends Renaud meant to exact, and did exact, from the licence he gave her to carry on an affair with Rézi. She finds Renaud and Rézi in the flat which Renaud had generously lent as a love-nest for the two women. And flees. The novel is written without any diary markings, but oscillates between the diary recounting of events ('last night...') and a strange, suspended present. Yet an already sophisticated control makes Claudine, in her carefree young bride moods of the beginning, voice a childlike sensuality that is a foundation for better things, and stands her in good stead in her day of need, at the end of the book. The quest that Colette is conducting through her heroine is of a more constructed kind than the earlier novels. Thus when Renaud offers his bride-to-be a ruby pendant (a strange gift, you might say), she sucks it like a sweet, 'because it must melt and smell of tangy raspberry!'. And so the following day Renaud brings her sweets. Which is, you might say, all part of your nymphette act, like the 'absinth-tasting' lollipops of *Claudine In Paris*. But it is more than this. Claudine is also asserting that she will not be bought, that value according to the world will not be allowed to efface her own 'primary' relish of life. And she won't buy the loaded symbolism, of the ruby: she thinks it's wine; or raspberry-coloured: *not* blood. She's still a child in a good sense: her sensations, her taste, are unspoilt. She will not learn the ways of the world. And so, when back in Montigny she opens the trunk Renaud has sent after her, she will not touch the ruby pendant in its green jewel-case. Nor taste the highly-sugared chocolates he's also sent, knowing now how bitter such gifts taste when the mouth is full of tears. But back in her darling woods, she relishes the full 'jouissance' to feel like a live animal, 'une brute vivace', 'accessible only to the savour of crusty bread, of a floury apple'. Her hunger for the landscape is of the same kind: 'those level dark woods smell of apple, the fresh bread is as cheerful as the pink tile roof which pierces them...' (*PL*: 522–3).

And that is really where recreated Claudine remains. She does resume life with Renaud, does also regain some of her androgyny, her foil-like, supple steel, lackadaisical charm in *Claudine and Annie* and *The Sentimental Retreat*.

Annie finds herself troubled by Claudine a little in the way in which Claudine was by Rézi: but it is Claudine's relation with the woods of Casamène, Annie's house, that draw from Colette her most inspired prose. The nymph has become a faun, she even dresses up as one in a pantomime: but she pursues no nymphs any more, she makes Claudine refuse Annie's advances...

There hangs around the *Claudine* and the *Minne*, despite the (already) exquisite writing about 'nature' and active, ever-moving bodies, a sense of being stuck with an ailing and arrested self. Claudine is made to fall ill twice, both times at crisis points in her orientation towards homosexuality or heterosexuality: just after she's moved to Paris and before she's met Renaud; and at a crucial stage in her affair with Rézi, when Renaud moves in on it. Minne also is ill after the failure of her bold expedition to leave her bourgeois home and become a gangster's moll. The tendrils of the vine, in the book by that name, are said to do precisely that to the nightingale that lets itself be overcome by the honey night: wind themselves around it, bind it, arrest its flight. The book is made up of short, poetic or conversational pieces: the former in particular ring like something between a song and a cry, the trapped nightingale's cry-like song. The speaker, who calls herself Colette as if it were a first name, writes about a woman lover whom she addresses as 'tu', or who addresses her as 'tu'. A genuine ambiguity hangs over those pieces. For in a sense, the woman lover who makes 'volupté' leap under the skin of the speaker's body, 'from her arched throat to her convulsed feet' is a *maternal* figure. With a hand 'dry, warm, slender as mountain lavender', she dispenses pleasure as a balm, a remedy against the torment of living, rocking the speaker to sleep, brooding over her anguish. She is also a twin sister whose body so merges with that of the speaker that the

white bed in which they sleep, too wide for one, too
narrow for two, only bears the imprint of one body in its
centre. And who can be confided in as another self:

> I belong to a country that I have left ... Come, you who do
> not know it, let me whisper to you: the scent of the woods in
> my country is equal to the strawberry and the rose! You
> could swear, when the thorn copses are in bloom, that a
> fruit is ripening you know not where – there, here, close
> by – an unseizable fruit that you breathe in by opening your
> nostrils. (*TV*: 968–974)

The speaker's country, with its magic, all-pervasive
and ungraspable fruit, is indeed an earthly paradise: but
its apple is innocence, relish of the primary senses, taste,
smell, like the woods and floury apple whose smell and
taste Claudine returns to at the end of *Claudine Married*. It
is not a fruit of knowledge, it knows neither good nor
evil. Still the evocation *is* ambiguous, for the speaker's
relation to her lover is ambiguous. The lover's country is
the sea, the grey, wind-sprayed sea. It is reality, the
present: Rozven, Missy's house in Brittany, if one wants
to feed biography into this piece. The speaker wants to
shelter into the past: the warm, fruit-scented, land-
locked world of her childhood. She is recalled from it by a
character who is a kind of double, but also at the same
time a reality principle. She draws the speaker back into
the real world, makes her re-enter the day, run through
the open doors and windows towards the dusk-gilt
beach, and pick the 'pink tortoiseshell petals' torn from
some 'imperishable flower' and that the waves scatter'
(*TV*: 976). *And* that sea-world which the lover offers is
maternal, while being overly, if delicately, *sexual*.

What I am trying to suggest, which is difficult to state,
so complex are the modes of *The Tendrils of the Vine*, is that

all these dual and suspended states convey, above all, a sense of suspended and bewildered identity. The lover is another self, merges into the speaker. The lover is a mother who nurses back into life her who is almost dying of pining for her lost childhood – just as Sido, the actual mother, had nursed the actual Colette back into life after her marriage. But because the lover is also a kind of twin, it is almost as if the speaker were nursing into existence her own maternal capacity... In a very real way, that is what Colette did: for her next heroine, a mature woman, a heroine who has suffered and is no longer burdened by nymphette requirements, unlike Claudine, is called Renée Nérée. Re-born Nereid, as it were. Born from the sea, a sea creature inhabiting the shady depths of the music-hall underground. Her name like a mirror too: Re-née/Né-rée. For in a sense, although, for the first time in Colette's work, a heroine makes a strong bid for independence, she is still caught in a suspended state. At the end of *The Vagabond*, Renée chooses freedom, an unmediated relation to the world. She renounces the man she loves not to lose that freedom. But in the sequel, *The Shackle*, she falls a fascinated prey to powerful and wayward Jean, ends the novel trapped, waiting, indoors... One could project onto the writing of that whole period of Colette's life, the period in which she was living with Missy and working in the music-hall, had abortive affairs then fell for Henry de Jouvenel, the strange vision that closes the piece 'The Mirror', in *The Tendrils of The Vine*. Colette has been visited by Claudine. Colette tries to fight free of Claudine, to assert her difference from Claudine, and in particular to emancipate her childhood from Claudine's. Claudine reminds her that she's been her mistress: Colette cut her hair off after Claudine did, to imitate Claudine... Not the last time Colette's fiction was to precede her life. But her 'dear double's' thought joins her own:

> Winged, united, dizzyingly they rise like the soft velvety owls of the greening twilight. Till what time will they suspend their flight without parting, above those two motionless, similar bodies, whose faces are being slowly devoured by night? (*TV*: 1033)

The return to the matrix, or the recreated body

Colette's writing of that period (1906–11 or so) is full of erasures and mysteries. She writes about music-hall *sidelights, L'Envers du music-hall,* its reverse side, but not about the show itself. Her writing, later on, about that period, *Chance Acquaintances, Gribiche, Rainy Moon, The Pure and The Impure,* will be the same, filled with blanks, the absence of love as a centre for living, and oscillations between various modes of selfhood.

One of the blanks, of 'envers', is that, from *Claudine and Annie* and *The Sentimental Retreat* onwards, and with the exception of the suggestive, but short and discreet pieces in *The Tendrils of the Vine,* Colette no longer writes about homosexual love. Or rather, she makes Claudine refuse to give Annie the pleasure she is craving for, she creates strongly heterosexual heroines from Renée and Mitsou onwards, even when there are powerful relations between her women, as between Jane and Fanny in *The Other One,* or the sisters in *The Toutonier.* Furthermore, in *The Pure and The Impure,* where she denounces Proust's portrayal of Gomorrah as way off the mark, and Gomorrah itself as pitifully small, sheltering in the nooks and crannies of Paris in the shadow of Sodom, its gigantic and all-pervasive counterpart, she speaks of lesbian love as a sisterly refuge against the hard world of men. We are very far from Claudine and Rézi, and even the motifs of *The Tendrils of the Vine* have suffered shrinkage. She almost blames the ladies of Llangdollen, who spent years of unruffled bliss in their cottage by the sea, for the evenness of their existence: as if the peace had driven the life away. She even hints that there was an imbalance in the relationship, that the powerful, diary-writing one throve at the expense of the other, who never wrote a line apart from one final, strange letter, thanking the giver for a gift of flowers and seeds, and only voicing her grief at her beloved friend's death in the language of flowers: 'I thank you for the seeds of Heartease, I only fear that they might be difficult to cultivate in these unfavourable times...' (*P & I*: 101)

The relationship with Missy is the most mysterious of Colette's long-lasting relationships.[10] One may well wonder why it is so, and whether some kind of suppression was at work, then or later. Complaining that the lesbian 'floats in space', Adrienne Rich describes her own 'searches through literature in the past, in pursuit of a flickering, often disguised reality which came and went through women's books'.[11] The reader of Colette, looking for traces of Missy, is in a similar state: all the heroines, fictional or autobiographical, from Renée to 'Colette' of the blank stories I mentioned earlier, are strikingly *single*. No trace of a companion. Lilian Federman, though she praises Colette for recognizing that 'the basis of lesbian love is not "bitter ectasy" or indiscriminate promiscuity but a bond that goes deeper than fleeting sexual passions' in *The Pure and The Impure*, still accuses her of not having been 'entirely free of the lesbian image promulgated by her literary predecessors.[12] Was it because a sensational view of lesbianism still was with Colette that she all but erased

Missy? Because the stigma of what had been a scandalous relationship was one she tried to efface in her later, respectable career as journalist and wife of baron Henry de Jouvenel? Because she felt guilty about the way she had dumped Missy after her affair with Jouvenel had started, and could not emotionally afford to take stock of what that relationship meant, or had meant? Because she changed so much in after years that she was no longer interested?

All of this may have been at work, but the heart of the matter seems to me to lie elsewhere. Colette herself, in *The Pure and The Impure* evokes the 'great and rare good faith', the 'noble modesty' that it takes for any woman to face up to what, in her, 'stumbles and tips over' from 'official' to 'clandestine' sexuality (*P & I*: 54). That word 'clandestine' is significant: for how to represent what is always misrepresented (even by Proust, even by Colette at the time of the *Claudine* since they were never free from that commercial, voyeuristic dimension) or deemed to be unrepresentable? How to represent what does not belong, or will not belong, to representation?[13] That is why the policy of writing 'blank' texts (like *Rainy Moon*, which will be discussed later) is so appropriate, in that they deal in an extraordinarily suggestive, guesswork way with gender and sexual ambiguities and with lesbian desire, or the possibility of lesbian desire. Perhaps we should accept that Colette literally means her reader to read between the lines.

For she did not suffer from inhibitions in relation to lesbianism. She had, after all, written the *Claudine*, she had unashamedly and cruelly drawn *Claudine Married* from her own affair with Georgie Raoul-Duval (who vainly tried to suppress the book). She had loving friendships with other women all her life, with Marguerite Moréno from the early 1900s to Marguerite's death, later with others, in particular Claude Chauvière. Even as a society hostess and later, as an old woman in her wheel-chair, she openly showed the appeal that other women's beauty had for her: she it was who spotted Audrey Hepburn in a hotel on the Riviera and chose her as her American Gigi. She remained friends with Natalie Clifford-Barney and others of those years till her death.

It seems to me that it is precisely because the relationship with Missy was important to her, because between 1906 and 1911 it had become the mainstay of her life that she was so protectively secretive about it: she could no longer be playful and exploitative as she had been in the *Claudine*, and the tribute of love is there in those poetic pieces of *The Tendrils of The Vine*. The protectiveness had to do with Missy's personality as well. The name 'La Chevalière' which she chose to give to her portrait of Missy in *The Pure and The Impure*, and which means the she-rider as well as the she-knight and a signet-ring, signals among other things Missy's love of horses, the fitful splendour that horse-riding gave to transvestites such as herself and that, Colette says, the motor car took away. But there was not only in Missy the aristocratic panache and reckless disregard of public opinion which led her to producing herself at the Moulin Rouge, there was also, as Colette makes clear, extreme vulnerability and a distaste for actual (as opposed to stage) limelight. Colette portrays her several cuts above the other transvestites in her circle as well as the women lovers who mercilessly exploited her, taking from her patronage, pleasure and money. 'Towering above a restless and debile court, her white, square forehead, her anxious, near-black eyes were seeking for what she never found: a calm emotional climate.' How could Colette have further exploited her by writing about her, about the lonely androgyne that she saw her as, the one who has no like, who has 'the right, and even the duty never to be happy' and who, Pierrot or seraph-like, is constantly wounded by her 'half-like', woman, who so fascinates her, in whom she pursues a mirage, in whose gaze she dreams of plunging and losing herself somewhere 'between the sea-weed and the star'? (P & I: 60–63)

There is something awful about the vulnerability Colette leads us to guess. She hints at children of aristocrats – I think one can confidently read, Missy – who were, in an earlier generation, dreadfully neglected by their parents, abandoned to the tender and untender mercies of the servants. They were, she hints, the victims of capricious care, sadistic punishments and sexual abuse. She also hints that in her relationships with women, Missy somehow was reproducing the patterns of her childhood: seeking love from her inferiors (morally this time as well as sexually), offering herself for punishment, in a quest perhaps for the maternal/paternal love she had never had. The woman who fled from a husband she hated and when she thought she needed an abortion only found comfort in the old valet who had abused her as a little girl and who whispered to her, while she was drinking the vile brew, the words of endearment he had used then, 'Niña –... Pobrecita...' (P & I: 59), perhaps only found that love through being maternal herself. And through her relationship with Colette.

What could document that relationship, Colette's letters to her mother, were destroyed by Achille after Sido's death: here one can indeed talk of suppression. Wonderfully, Sido's letters to Colette have survived, now published by *Editions des femmes*. They shadow forth a Missy far different from the sad, flamboyant transvestite that survives in the photographs as Arab horseman, Roman emperor, monk or sea-captain. Sido treats Missy as the ordinary, evidently kind companion to her daughter that she was. 'Amitiés à Missy', love to Missy, is the invariable end to her letters, and gradually, as she feels how good, how protective, how generous Missy is being to Minet-Chéri, it changes to 'Tendresses à Missy'. She includes Missy in her enquiries about the women's health or their latest venture with one of those new, dangerous objects, a motor car, she sends them 'galette' or water-chestnuts, sends Missy some fresh country eggs and is surprised and delighted to see them return, hand-painted by Missy. Sido, from her own admission, did not care about what the world calls 'morals', but she cared greatly about her daughter's happiness and well-being – was appalled when that stabilizing relationship broke off and Jouvenel appeared on the scene. Everything that transpires from Sido's letters suggests that Missy had almost found in her life with Colette (despite the absences that arose from Colette's music-hall career, her tours of the provinces), that 'calm emotional climate' she was dreaming about. And that she lost for ever when Colette left her. It meant she also lost Sido, that distant but welcoming mother-figure whose humble country gifts must have made up for the neglect of her own aristocratic parents.... She in turn had mothered Colette....

Perhaps all those years later in *The Pure and The Impure* Colette's account of the ladies of Llangdollen, her dreamy contemplation of the narrow white bed in which they slept (which to me recalls the bed of *The Tendrils of the Vine*) is Colette's way of saying what there was in her friendship with Missy, and also why she left her. Her impatience with the limitations, the seclusion, even the peace of their life may explain, as well as be an

attempt to justify her sudden departure. For there are
parallels. Like Lady Eleanor Butler, Missy was rich, was
high-born. Like Sarah Ponsonby, Colette was relatively
poor and low-born. But it was Colette who acted,
Colette who wrote, it was Missy who could have
complained that the seeds of heartsease would not grow.
Missy the generous, who used to say that the role of the
donator is overvalued in medieval paintings, gave
Rozven, the house in Brittany, to Colette. Missy was
ruined by her lovers, she died derelict and alone after a
bungled attempt at suicide. Colette was recreated,
mothered back into life, by the friendship.

In some ways rather like Missy, the music-hall seems
to have functioned for Colette as a matrix, a world of
transvestism and *apparent* flamboyance, in which the
artists shared a strong sense of sisterly or brotherly
companionship, as Renée does with Braque. *The Vagabond,
Music-Hall Sidelights, Gribiche, Mitsou* even, reveal a sad,
big-hearted, recklessly impecunious or prodigal world,
in which people help each other against a background of
insecurity and fatalism. Through that world Colette
regained, not a voice (unlike coughing Dora, her
problem was not speech), but a language rooted in the
body. Miming was learning to speak without words, but
with the whole body. The reverse of hysteria. Rooting
speech in physicality, Colette was 're-born': her Re-née
speaks with a voice that has a new freshness, a new
dynamism, above all, an unprecedented directness. At
the same time, Colette also seems to have been regaining
sexual power, recharging a formidable libido that was to
become unleashed from the meeting with Jouvenel
onwards.

There is a great difference between Claudine's
loving – however vivid and wild – and Renée's attraction
to, and flight from, love. There is, in Renée, as well as a

capacity for adult passion, the deep knowledge of one who has suffered and cannot trust again and thinks she cannot be moved again – and yet who longs for, needs love as she would life. Claudine's first kiss mixes resistance and pleasure: she does not know whether she 'se cabre ou se cambre', is rearing up or arching her back. There is the same pattern to Renée's kiss with Maxime, but the reverberations are of quite another order:

> For the lips that kiss me are just the same as yesterday, gentle, cool, and impersonal, and their ineffectiveness irritates me. But all of a sudden they change, and now I no longer recognize the kiss, which quickens, insists, falters, then begins again with a rhythmical movement, and finally stops as if waiting for a response which does not come.
> I move my head imperceptibly, because of his moustache which brushes against my nostrils with a scent of vanilla and honeyed tobacco. Oh!... Suddenly my mouth, in spite of itself, lets itself be opened, opens of itself as irresistibly as a ripe plum splits in the sun. And once again there is born that exacting pain that spreads from my lips, all down my flanks as far as my knees, that swelling as of a wound that wants to open once more and overflow – the voluptuous pleasure that I had forgotten.
> (V: 107)

Renée escapes from the enclosure that she feels Maxime's love to be: 'I refuse to see the most beautiful countries of the world microscopically reflected in the amorous mirror of your eyes.' No 'she for God in him' for the Vagabond: she chooses an unmediated relation to things. But The Shackle, a sequel also written in the form of a journal, and also posing questions of sexuality and liberty, finds Renée recognizing that vagabondage is 'no substitute for self-renewal'. A new love reduces her to a state of mesmerized pliancy: a 'reflection in someone else's mirror', Jean comes to her from behind in the hall of their Geneva hotel, kisses her on the nape of the neck:

> A good kiss, warm, not too devouring; warm, long and tranquil; a kiss that took time to satisfy itself and that gave me, after the first shiver down my spine, a slightly lethargic contentment.[14]

After Maxime, and after Jean, there is the blue lieutenant, who reveals love to Mitsou, makes their coupled shapes on Mitsou's bed cast on the walls the shadow of a wonderful gallop... and who leaves Mitsou. And then, there is Chéri.

Out of the looking-glass: Chéri

If one compares Léa's first kiss with Chéri with the kisses above, it is evident, not just that a powerful, almost triumphant erotic assurance has been reached, but also that the voice of the author has gained a similar assurance: not just because she is, for the first time in a major fiction, writing in the third, instead of the first person:

> She went to kiss him, on an impulse of resentment and selfishness, and half thinking to chastise him. 'Just you wait, my boy.... It's all too true that you've a pretty mouth, and, this time, I'm going to take my fill because I want to – and then I'll leave you, I don't care what you may say. Now...'
> Her kiss was such that they reeled apart, drunk, deaf, breathless, trembling as if they had just been fighting. She stood up again in front of him, but he did not move from the depths of his chair, and she taunted him under her breath, 'Well?... Well?' and waited for an insult. Instead, he held

out his arms, opened his vague beautiful hands, tilted his head back as if he had been struck, and let her see beneath each eyelash the glint of a shining tear. He babbled indeterminate words – a whole animal chant of desire, in which she could distinguish her name – 'darling' – 'I want you' – 'I'll never leave you' – a song to which she listened, solicitous, leaning over him, as if unwittingly she had hurt him to the quick. (*Chéri*: 36)

Chéri is the son of an ageing, wealthy courtesan. Leá, a friend of his mother's, takes him in hand, and they have a wonderful affair. Léa suffers when she thinks she's lost Chéri who's got married to a 'suitable', wealthy young wife. But when she gets him back, she confronts her own ageing, and at dawn she sends Chéri away.

Later, Colette was to call Chéri 'symphonic'. A character born out of those music-haunted years she had spent as the wife of Willy. The wife of a fast-ageing husband, a young bride who had never known the taste and smell of a young man's flesh. She had had the revelation of how exquisite that could be, one day Polaire, close to her own face, had kissed handsome Pierre Louÿs.

Chéri was the first work Colette felt confident about. She had been delighted by Francis Jammes's admiration for *Creature Conversations*, and by Proust's enthusing letter about *Mitsou*. With *Chéri*, she did not need the reassurance. And it is her first work that cannot easily be rooted into autobiography.

Certainly, you could say that Colette had known the world of courtesans in the pre-war years. That in ageing Léa's dramatic renunciation to love, there was the projection of Colette's own fear of ageing: she was nearing fifty – Léa is forty-nine at the beginning of the novel, then passes the threshold of fifty – and, in *The Last of Chéri*, the sequel written three years later, she has become an old woman, almost virile in her sexlessness. Colette herself had put on weight during her pregnancy – little Colette de Jouvenel had been born in 1912 – was giving vent more and more to her relish for good food and wine, and was well on her way to the thirteen stone she was to reach. Yet, in so far as autobiography is about the past and involves a retrospective mode, *Chéri* cannot be classed as such. It was *imagined*, projected as a *gestalt*, as it were, in a way none of Colette's previous works had been. There is a forgetfulness of self as narrator in the writing of *Chéri*, which is paralleled by Léa's own relation to her mirror-images. It is no longer Colette being trapped by her 'double' Claudine, nor Renée seeking to free herself from the necessary mirror of a loved man's gaze. Léa has a vision of herself in the future through having a vision of others. Walking in the garden of Chéri's mother, Charlotte, she hears her say, 'here comes the happy pair', and rushes back towards the house, thinking Chéri and his bride are back from their honeymoon, prepared to see them framed in the doorway. Instead, she finds 70-year-old Lili mincing with her young lover, like a caricature of herself and Chéri. Back home, she shivers with anguish as if with fever:

> She was obsessed by the vision of an empty doorway, with clumps of red salvia on either side. 'I can't be well,' she thought, 'one doesn't get into a state like this over a door!' Again she saw the three old women, Lili's neck . . . (*Chéri*: 60)

She has had a warning vision of her own fate. It catches up with her at the end of the book, when she's sent Chéri away. She watches him leave her path, walk into the morning air as if just escaped from prison. For a minute she thinks he's going to retrace his steps:

'He's coming back! He's coming back!' she cried, raising her arms.

An old woman, out of breath, repeated her movements in the long pier-glass, and Léa wondered what she could have in common with that crazy creature. (*Chéri*: 136)

Léa's release of Chéri has the effect of releasing her own trapped self, of making her come out of the mirror. *The Last of Chéri* finds her jocose, robust, reconciled to life. It is Chéri, branded by World War I, who cannot get over his pining for the Léa of the past. Colette herself from *Chéri* onwards seems to be free from writing about 'experience', writing in a diary mode.

For *Chéri* was anticipation. It announced a crisis Colette had not yet encountered. It portrayed the love between a mature woman and a very young man: a love Colette had never known, but had dreamt about. In *Chéri*, fiction *precedes* life. Then life took over. Colette gave her adolescent stepson, Bertrand (whom she had invited to spend the summer with her, little Colette and their half-brother Renaud in Rozven) a copy of *Chéri*. On the inside page, she wrote: 'A mon fils CHERI, Bertrand', incorporating the title in the dedication, identifying Chéri with a son and Bertrand with Chéri. It was that summer that she started an affair with Bertrand. There had been play among the women there – Germaine Beaumont, Colette – about who should, in true Balzac tradition, initiate the young man. Rumour has it that the choice fell on Germaine Beaumont, but that Bertrand, terrified, sought refuge in Colette's bedroom.

Colette had written that scene twice already: between Léa and Chéri, and in *The Sentimental Retreat*, where Marcel, Claudine's homosexual stepson, is supposed to go and satisfy Annie. He can't go through with it, and Annie seeks solace in Colette's arms. Only, Claudine does not... With Bertrand, Colette did. And as the relationship with Bertrand seems to have been suggested by *Chéri*, so *The Ripening Seed* grew out of the relationship. Fiction weaves in and out of life, life imitates or flows from, fiction. The relation between the two has ceased to be chronological or hierarchical. It would make no sense to speak of 'realism' about Colette. More as if life and fiction were two seas, separate but interflowing through some mysterious straits, like the Atlantic and the Mediterranean. But Hercules' pillars no longer mark the limits of a bounded world, and no one knows through what eddies and currents the two seas communicate with each other.

Colette herself, in years to come, was to move from the Atlantic to the Mediterranean. From one sea to another. From Rozven to La Treille Muscate. From one dark young man, Bertrand, to another, Maurice: older, and there to stay. Her fiction seems to be in the business of seeking the conditions for life to go on too. One of these is learning to renounce. She tries it in *Chéri*. Léa gives up Chéri as a gesture of grace, the heroic actress of a drama Chéri himself does not understand. Madame Dalleray in *The Ripening Seed* goes away, having realized that she is 'the beggar' in the affair with young Philippe. The need to renounce, and finding the grace to renounce, are central to a book Colette was to write ten years later, *The Break of Day*. When she wrote it, she herself had not renounced. She was in the middle of a passionate affair with Goudeket. Yet there is a progress from one book to another in understanding what kind of love makes renunciation possible. And that is, maternal love.

Colette had known motherhood with the birth of Bel-Gazou, soon after her own mother's death. She had also known fullness of adult passion through her love for

Jouvenel, however much she suffered from it. Her fictional men, from Jean to Farou to Michel to D'Espivant, are substantial in a way Renaud was not, as if the author's engagement with her man enabled her to body forth male creatures. In Colette, it is not a question of language being born from the death or frustration of desire, as with Mallarmé's faun, but of language being born all the better as desire is fulfilled. Jouvenel was less ambiguously male than Willy had been. He seems to have ballasted a side of her nature, enabled her to come to terms with her own androgyny by satisfying something in her that wanted to be vulnerable and possessed. Missy, before him, had created or re-created in Colette a throbbing susceptibility that was very different from the insolent verve of tomboy Claudine. But that womanliness had been a thing of the shade. Claudine and Colette's hovering souls are owls, night beasts. Renée's soul is not obscure, she claims, but dark: 'made beautiful by an unwearying sadness; silvery and twilit like the white owl, the silky mouse, the wings of the clothes moth'. Léa is also half a creature of the night: but she is regally decisive, and the mirror-images she wrestles with are outdoors. Daylight, sea-light, are triumphant in *The Ripening Seed*. I think this is owing to a blossoming of physicality that has to do with mothering.

Colette was not a good mother. She wrote very movingly about Bel-Gazou. But she was ironic about her pregnant state, comparing herself to a 'bloated rat', and the little girl was looked after by others, an English nurse in particular, from the beginning. Later she was sent to boarding-school, which is unusual in France. The presence of Bel-Gazou in Rozven did not stop Colette from conducting the affair with Bertrand, Bel-Gazou's step-brother and playing companion. Who knows but that, later, Bel-Gazou's failed marriage to an older man, her discreet and it seems not very happy homosexuality, her withdrawal and silence, did not come from an unappeased love, from having found her mother wanting? Renaud de Jouvenel, Bel-Gazou's other step-brother and companion, never forgave...

In 'human' or 'moral' terms, Colette was greedy, was ruthless. She sacrificed her real daughter. A knowing Jocasta, she seduced Oedipus. But the breaking of the taboo, the fulfilment of the mother's incestuous wish for the son (as little Sido's incestuous wish for the father had been magically fulfilled), enabled an extraordinary imaginative, mothering power, to be born in Colette. She got what she deeply wanted, what is forbidden: and getting it, she began to develop the power to let go. The amazing dedication of *Chéri* to Bertrand welcomed him into a world in which an ageing woman knows her greatest passion for a man who could be her son, and gives him up: because a love even greater than the first, because maternal love, takes over. 'I have kept you close to my heart too long,' Léa says to Chéri. 'I have kept you close to my heart too long, Minet-Chéri,' are the words which, later, Colette will place in her own mother's mouth. From the beginning, not knowing yet what she was doing, Colette had placed her relationship with Bertrand in the shadow of Sido. When Bertrand first visited his stepmother, he shyly withdrew into a corner. Colette came into the room, could not see him. 'Where is the child?' she said: the very words that she makes Sido speak at the beginning of *My Mother's House*: 'Where are the children?'

Colette wrote *My Mother's House* because Bertrand had asked her to show him the house and the village of Saint-Sauveur, because she kept telling him stories about her childhood. As the *Claudine* novels had been born from the father/master's desire that she narrate those youthful days, so *La Maison de Claudine*, redeemingly, is born from the adoptive son's desire to be told about 'the mother'. It is as if Bertrand had given Colette the imaginatively satisfying motherhood that she wanted. And doing so, after she had already had the imaginative revelation of what that could be, through the character of Léa, the floodgates that had, up till then, kept her own childhood distant from her, a country to which she still belonged, but which she had left, were opened.

She had become the mother, where it mattered, for her, as a writer. She had become her own mother. Spoken, written, words her mother had spoken. Her mother would ever remain ahead of her: the imaginary world was ahead of reality. But she could try and get ever closer to it.

Henry de Jouvenel, Theseus-like, had plenty of affairs. Unlike Hippolytus, Bertrand, the stepson, was glad to be seduced. But there is no denying the accusation that Sylvain Bonmariage, the vitriolic champion of Willy in those years, threw at Colette: she had, without any compunction, committed what Racine's Phaedra feels damned for even *wishing* to do: adultery compounded by incest. But perhaps it is only when taboos function so as to regulate exchanges between men that incest of the 'symbolic' kind Colette committed (Bertrand was her stepson, not her son) seems so wicked? The 'darling' son, 'chéri' as 'Minet-Chéri' had been by Sido, was giving Colette her mother back. It does not make sense, for the Colette tribe, to argue with Freud that the child is the 'penis' the father gives to the little girl. It was distinctively a little daughter, that could be kept close to the heart, that Sido had cherished. And it was her mother that lover/son Bertrand gave to Colette. The figures of the Oedipus and the castration complex go on helplessly buzzing, like a master computer jammed by a clever question, when you try to apply Freudian categories to Colette.

What does woman want?[15] Everything, Colette answers. The mother, the father, the sister, the brother, the son. Wanting the son is wanting to be the mother. The figure in the mirror is ahead now: in the future.

Are you imagining, as you read me, that I'm portraying myself? Have patience: this is merely my model (*B of D: 5*)

Chapter Seven

The Mother's Houses

Curiosity is supposed to be woman's capital fault. It led Eve to taste the fruit and give it to Adam. Pandora cannot stop herself from prying: she opens the box that releases misfortunes upon mankind. Balzac's *A Daughter of Eve* has the heroine almost cuckold her husband, so keen is she to discover what love is.

Sido disapproved of curiosity, especially sexual curiosity. But she had her own version, which tallies with none of the traditional ones. She saw it as a wrongful impatience, a yearning to destroy:

> Two warm walls formed an angle which kept the harsh winds from her trial-ground, which consisted of some red earthenware bowls in which I could see nothing but loose, dormant earth.
> 'Don't touch!'
> 'But nothing's coming up!'
> 'And what do you know about it? Is it for you to decide?'

But Sido cannot remember what is buried: crocus bulbs,

117

or a chrysalis? She stops her daughter's hand that wants to scratch the earth: 'Don't touch!' Otherwise the air, the light, will shrivel the life. Yet she, like her own daughter, is possessed by the powerful curiosity of the treasure-seeker, the need to 'lay bare and bring to light something that no human eye' has before gazed upon. All she can do is call her daughter an 'eight-year-old murderess':

> She knew that I should not be able to resist, any more than she could, the desire to know, that like herself I should ferret in the earth of that flowerpot until it had given up its secret. I never thought of our resemblance, but she knew I was her own daughter and that, child though I was, I was already seeking for the sense of shock, the quickened hear-beat, and the sudden stoppage of the breath – symptoms of the private ecstasy of the treasure-seeker. (*Sido*: 152–4)

Sido saw her daughter's curiosity about sex, her need to run away from home, run away to man, wander about the world, as a kind of original sin. Not the sin of disobeying God's law. The sin of betraying the mother. Minet-Chéri, The Little One, has boasted to her village friends that she wants to be a sailor, know travel and adventure. Then a lamp glows red behind the sitting-room window, and the child is suddenly aware of the evening damp:

> The garden, grown suddenly hostile, menaces a now sobered little girl with the cold leaves of its laurels, the raised sabres of its yuccas, and the barbed caterpillars of its monkey-puzzle tree. A roar like the ocean comes from the direction of Moutiers where the wind, unchecked, runs in flurries over the tossing treetops. The Little One, sitting on the grass, keeps her eyes fixed on the lamp, veiled for a moment by a brief eclipse. A hand has passed in front of the

flame, a hand wearing a shining thimble. At the mere sight
of this hand the Little One starts to her feet, pale, gentle
now, trembling slightly as a child must who for the first
time ceases to be the happy little vampire that unconsciously drains the maternal heart; trembling slightly at the
conscious realization that this hand and this flame, and the
bent, anxious head beside the lamp, are the centre and the
secret birthplace whence radiate in ripples ever less
perceptible, in circles ever more and more remote from the
essential light and its vibrations, the warm sitting-room
with its flora of cut branches and its fauna of peaceful
creatures; the echoing house, dry, warm, and crackling as a
newly baked loaf; the garden, the village.... Beyond these
all is danger, all is loneliness.

The 'sailor' with faltering steps, ventures upon *terra firma*
and makes for the house, turning her back on an enormous
yellow moon, just rising. Adventure? Travels? The
enterprise that makes the emigrant? With her eyes glued
to the shining thimble, to the hand that passes to and fro
before the flame, Minet-Chéri savours the delicious
contrition of being – like the clockmaker's child, like the
little girls of the laundress and the baker – a child of her
village, hostile alike to colonist and barbarian, one of those
whose universe is bounded by the limits of a field, by the
entrance of a shop, by the circle of light spreading beneath a
lamp, and crossed at intervals by a well-loved hand drawing
a thread and wearing a silver thimble. (*My M's H:*
39–40)

Here the movement of the mother's thimble draws the
child back to her. Later on, The Little One, now herself a
mother, teaches her daughter Bel-Gazou to sew:

it would seem that with this needle-play she has
discovered the perfect means of adventuring, stitch by
stitch, point by point, along a road of risks and temptations.
Silence... the hand armed with the steel dart moves back

and forth. Nothing will stop the unchecked little explorer.
At what moment must I utter the 'Halt!' that will brutally
arrest her in full flight? (ibid: 132)

Bel-Gazou's reverie is the escape into sex, away from
the mother: a premise of puberty. Colette, however
inadequate she feels, confronted with her daughter's
curiosity, claims that 'it is wise to tremble, to be silent
and to lie when one draws near to 'that most majestic
and disturbing of instincts'. She lets Bel-Gazou off. She
remembers that in the days in which mothers kept
daughters tied to their apron-strings – or rather, as she
is speaking of aristocratic ladies, close to their skirts –
clever repressed girls like Balzac's Rosalie de Watteville
embroidered the loss and despair of a man on their
canvasses. Yet, in the earlier sailor passage, Sido does
keep her daughter. Indeed, the passage is ambiguous. It
is the mother whose lamp, inside the house, is red.
There is a coincidence between the lighting of the lamp
and the terror that sweeps over the garden, as if the one
triggered the other. And it is true that Colette would
never have become Colette if she had not had the
wanderer's instinct, and left her mother. The other
children had trouble growing up. Juliette, the elder sister
who used to hide inside her tented hair reading novels,
had a disastrous marriage and committed suicide. Of
the 'Sauvages', the boys, the one did not survive his
mother's death, the other never got over his longing for
childhood.

There is something dual about the figure of Sido. The
good mother that she was carried a 'bad' mother about
herself, perhaps the one who lights the red lamp, or the
one who lures her daughter to burdensome homosexual
desires. She sends her with a bunch of double
columbines to the house of her strange friend with the

yellow gipsy eyes, nomadic Adrienne. She encourages the 'wandering' taste that in another way she denies. Adrienne's house, unlike Sido's, is untidy, buried in flowery creepers. It is filled like that of a fairy-tale witch with 'piles of books all falling apart, mushrooms picked at dawn, wild strawberries, fossilized ammonites', even truffles. Sido and Adrienne suckled their infants at the same time, and once changed babies for fun. So laughingly Adrienne challenges Colette with a 'you whom I once fed with my own milk!' and Colette blushes, tormented, under Sido's clear but threatening gaze, by the image of 'Adrienne's swarthy breast and its hard, purple knob'. Although Adrienne never entices nor detains the child, she associates Adrienne and her dwelling with 'the idea of a first seduction' (*Sido*: 162–3).

You would think that Colette here touches upon Melanie Klein's distinction between the 'good' and the 'bad' breast. There is only one mother for Klein, but the child sometimes perceives her as nurturing, sometimes as aggressive (as he/she projects his/her own aggressive impulses onto her). But Sido and Adrienne do not fall into those categories. Nor does the child Colette whom Colette is recreating even begin to enter the nefarious kingdom of paranoid schizophrenia. Both mothers are real women, both nurture, and both threaten. Both have suckled the child, both are held in awe by her, Adrienne as a seductive gypsy goddess, Sido as the perceptive, 'blade-grey'-eyed decipherer of her secret moods. But also, with blissful distinctiveness, there are *two* mothers, and *two* houses. Not one, that would split into 'good' and 'bad' as if she were the one-eyed smithy god, Vulcan. Nor do the two mothers have two heads and one body, like the Virgin and St Anne in da Vinci's picture, who, according to Freud, represent the two mothers da Vinci had, the real and the adoptive, merging at the waist.

Adrienne's house and body are different from Sido's house and body. Yet in some respects they are alike. In Adrienne's house there is a black tom-cat with a white mask called Colette, and it eats plain chocolate. Marauding cats on a chocolate roof are part of Sido's child-lore. Yet Adrienne is a fauness, a rover. Sido eventually feels her to be a threat. As if she were a man, who could run away with her daughter, turn into the King of Hades.

Indeed the distinction between primary and secondary sexuality becomes active here. Colette protrays Sido as friendly to people who act a motherly part: like Adrienne, until her daughter begins to look troubled, and guilty. Like Missy. On the other hand, exotic women and powerful men alike are in her books the enemies of the mother. In *The Break of Day*, she explains to her daughter, once divorced and now proud of her new, handsome and clever husband, 'It's not so much divorce I mind, it's the marriage. It seems to me that almost anything would be better than marriage.' Why didn't Colette marry her other suitor, who was stupid? 'What beautiful things you'd write with the idiot, Minet-Chéri! With the other, you'll spend your time giving him all your most precious gifts' (29–30). Yet Colette did not fully believe what she makes her mother say. Choosing high-powered men, she was putting yeast into her life. Trouble, but in the long run and whatever else she might say, creative trouble. Still, it took years to negotiate between the instinct to run back to her mother, and that which made the little land-locked Burgundy girl dream of becoming a sailor. Renée the Vagabond's choice of the wide world is a major turning-point, though a contradictory and contradicted one. Later, Colette will encourage her young explorer friend *Renée* Hamon, the 'corsair', in her brave voyage. She will become a keen traveller herself: the sea in Brittany, the sea in Provence, sailing in a balloon, North Africa, New York... Bed-ridden in the Palais-Royal, she will dream of distant lands, the valley in the West Indies which, she's been told, blossoms into total and perfect pink for three days in the year.

But Sido had not just been the silver thimble, the magnet that draws the hidden child in the foliage. Sido was ever active, in the house, in the garden. The forbidden fruit she coveted were neither sex not knowledge. She had known great love with the Captain,[1] and had inexhaustible lore. But when age and illness overtook her, she longed for the activities that had been hers all life long:

> The forbidden fruits were the over-heavy bucket drawn up from the well, the firewood split with a bill-hook on an oaken block, the spade, the mattock, and above all the double steps propped against the gable-window of the wood-house.
>
> Burnt by the fire, cut with the pruning knife, soaked by melting snow or spilt water, she had always managed to enjoy her best moments of independence before the earliest risers had opened their shutters. (*My M's H:* 126)

Sido encourages her daughter to enjoy the delights of dawn, to wander through the woods, tasting of the springs whose savour she will never forget:

> At half past three everything slumbered in a primal blue, blurred and dewy... She would let me go, watching her creation – her masterpiece, as she said, grow smaller as I ran down the slope...
>
> I came back... not before I had described a great circle in the woods... and tasted the water of the two hidden springs that I worshipped. One of them bubbled out of the ground with a crystalline spurt and a sort of sob, and then

carved its own sandy bed. But it was no sooner born than it lost confidence and plunged underground again. The other spring, almost invisible, brushed over the grass like a snake, and spread itself out secretly in the middle of a meadow where the narcissus, flowering in a ring, alone bore witness to its presence. The first spring tasted of oak-leaves, the second of iron and hyacinth stalks . . . (*Sido*: 148)

A taboo-less god who grants dawn to her creation as a reward, lets her roam freely and taste of all the fruit and springs of her domain, even the most secret, the most symbol-laden one – a Demeter-Ceres who at that time fears no snakes in the grass, no seducers of her daughter, Sido is the one who *invites* her children to 'look', and know. She teaches them the names of creatures, plants, animals, trees. She is the lighter of fires and the cook of morning chocolate, practical, unromantic, as cunning and contrary as her children. She knows her daughter has put chestnuts in the ashes that are used to get the linen clean, and that the chestnuts will stain the linen. She knows her children's tricks and their manners. She too has a passionate curiosity, though she is more innocent than her daughter:

> In her life there was never the memory of a dishonoured wing, and if she trembled with longing in the presence of a closed calyx, a chrysalis still rolled in its varnished cocoon, at least she respectfully awaited the moment. How pure are those who have never forced anything open! (*B of D*: 25)

Up at dawn before everyone, Sido is portrayed as dreaming, like her sailor-daughter, to be 'an unchallengeable explorer' every morning when 'the cold dew seems to be falling, with little irregular plops, from the beaks of blackbirds' (ibid: 26). She loves all unusual or grand phenomena. She has known a 'rain of frogs' as some people have experienced clouds of grasshoppers, and her daughter in her turn will know, in Fez, a 'flood of nightingales', drunk at dawn on the brandied cherries which local people hang for them in walnut shells on the trees.[2] Sido it is who enjoys nothing so much as a glorious fire, even though it is the neighbour's barn that is burning: she sits over breakfast and watches it. Sido is all this, in Colette: a woman who does, and tells, and delights in life. She is not the still point of a still centre. Indeed, even the thimble is active, it darts in and out, light strikes the silvery cap. The mother's house is not bound by its walls. It is 'the central point of a Mariner's Chart of gardens, winds and rays of light, no section of which quite lay beyond my mother's influence'. In French, 'une rose de jardins, de vents, de rayons'. 'Une rose des vents', literally 'a rose of the winds', is a compass-card, divided into thirty-two petal-like segments. But the phrase, in French, is beautifully evocative, gathering all the wonderful symbolism of the rose with the notion of winds furling and unfurling, creating patterns in their eddies – as I believe they do. Sido is on various wave-lengths with the weather, she watches for signs and portents, she can tell from the way plants shiver or insects fold their wings whether it's going to rain or not:

> Sido and my childhood were both, and because of each other, happy at the centre of that imaginary star whose eight points bear the names of the cardinal and collateral points of the compass. (*Sido:* 163)

Sido was originally planned with the subtitle: 'ou les quatre points cardinaux', 'or the four cardinal points'. 'Cardinal' comes from 'cardo', pivot in Latin, and the name of one of the two axes on which cities were built. The cardinal points are the points on the horizon, defining an orientation in relation to the vertical plane that contains the rotation axis of the celestial sphere: the lines of the poles (I am quoting from the *Larousse*). What is striking about that whole idea of Sido, and Colette's childhood as she recreates it with and through Sido, is the combination of solidity and mobility. It is a system of balances and orientations, and it serves to navigate. Colette will put her utmost skill into reading the signs and portents in a Provençal storm, in *Bella-Vista*, as she will in reading the signs that should help her, as narrator or protagonist, interpret human feelings and make sense of human behaviour. It will never be judged or defined according to a *system* of beliefs.[3]

The lore Sido passed on from the centre of her house was not static, not the weight of an inheritance, the law the father lays upon the son, like Mr Tulliver's testament of vengeance to Tom in *The Mill on the Floss*. It is a readiness to do, and be. It is turned towards others, the future, and Colette will use it to energize her present. It also subverts the distinction between 'home' and 'the streets': the nineteenth-century housewife/harlot dichotomy. For Sido's house took in seduced girls and stray cats, and through its on-going exchanges with the neighbours, the village, the woods, the weather, it extended to the world, had no fixed boundaries. The walls, the garden walls, are the visible and reassuring signs of the innermost centrifugal eddies, like the markings on a compass-card. Sido may be nothing, a provincial housewife, in the world's eye. But there are no limits to which she will not soar:

> In those moments while it was still night my mother used to sing, falling silent as soon as anyone was able to hear. The

lark also sings while it is mounting towards the palest, least inhabited part of the sky. My mother climbed too, mounting carelessly up the ladder of the hours, trying to possess the beginning of the beginning.

There is something metaphysical, or mystical, in Sido's return to paradise, as if she were the first woman:

what she sought was a red, horizontal ray, and the pale sulphur that comes before the red ray; she wanted the damp wing that the first bee stretches out like an arm. The summer wind, that springs up at the approach of the sun, gave her its first-fruits in scents of acacia and woodsmoke; when a horse pawed the ground and whinnied softly in the neighbouring stable, she was the first to hear it. On an autumn morning she was the only one to see herself reflected in the first disk of ephemeral ice in the well-bucket, before her nail cracked it. (*B of D*: 26)

'I know what that particular intoxication is like,' Colette writes in the middle of this passage. Yet it took her a long time to recapture it. Not for the reasons which made Proust's remembrance of Combray so painstaking, not because the mother and house (lost in the financial fiasco) had sunk away in time. Sido after all had gone on living till 1912, writing to her daughter almost daily, still housing her daughter's animals, sending her gifts. But the bond had been ruptured by the marriage to Willy, and the search for identity, as well as the need to conceal her misery to spare Sido, who had as it was such a share of grief: her husband's death, her daughter Juliette's suicide, the sons' difficult lives, Colette's divorce, money worries. More importantly perhaps, Colette *had* to break the bond, if she was to find fulfilment. Sido's possessiveness of her children had something destructive about it. Colette describes her restless worry about Achille who had become exceedingly good-looking as the one moment when her mother had looked 'diminished': 'wild, full of false gaiety, given to malediction, ordinary, plain-looking and on the alert' (B of D: 25).

For years, imaginatively, through her heroines (Claudine, Annie, Renée) Colette oscillated between the flight 'back home' and freedom. I have suggested that her growing confidence had to do with her having a new matrix in the love of Missy, and music-hall companionship. If there are originally two mothers, Sido and Adrienne, a second couple of mothers (Sido and Missy) seems to have combined in that period to help Colette repair the damage she had suffered. Indeed, as I have already stressed, for I think it is important, Missy gave Rozven to Colette. It will be her first real house, a house of her own, in which she will create something like the home that Sido had made for her family: hospitable, wayward, cheerful. In that house Colette loved Jouvenel, enjoyed Bel-Gazou, in that house, which you could call the *second* mother's house, she came to love Bertrand. The house also 'engendered' *Le Blé en herbe* ('green corn', rather than 'the ripening seed' as it is translated: the stress is on love being at the shooting, not the ripening stage): Colette's portrayal, not just of seascapes and a life by the sea she had never attempted before, but her first imaginatively *detached* and totally 'clean' creation of adolescents.

Certainly, there are elements of Colette's affair with Bertrand in the 'amours' of the lady in white and sixteen-year-old Philippe. Including the Hitchcock-like signature of her being called Mme Dalleray: the street in Paris in which Hélène Picard had lent Colette and Bertrand her studio as a love-nest was called 'rue d'Alleray'. But the lady in white remains shadowy, seen almost entirely through Philippe, her needs and grief deep and understated. The focus is on the adolescents, and in particular fifteen-year-old Vinca, Vinca with her name of periwinkle, Vinca who is blue, not white like the lady, and has blue eyes like Colette's own daughter Bel-Gazou. Vinca, blue like the paper Colette writes on, and whose name suggests victory (as well as chain?): *vaincra*. Vinca reconquers Philippe. In her strange prescience and power and endurance, in her ability to go for what she wants, she is the equal of the lady-in-white. It is as if Colette had found in that fictional narrative alliance with the character of an adolescent girl the complicity with the daughter she had betrayed in real life. As if she wanted to give her the victory fictionally, empathized with the gangly, wise little housewife whom in real life she exiled to boarding-school.

It is as if, through her gift of a house by the sea, abandoned Missy was continuing to mother Colette imaginatively, enabling her to come to the fulfilment of motherhood. As if one woman was inside another and in her turn, as with Russian dolls, housed another. Vinca inside Colette inside Missy. Bertrand inside Colette inside Sido. The love for Bertrand gave Colette her mother back, made possible for her the return to the Saint-Sauveur house, the return to Claudine's childhood that Claudine herself could never effect. From inside that house, she could teach Bel-Gazou to sew as Sido had taught her to sew. With that daughter, she continued the rivalry that had been imaginatively begun between Léa and Edmée, Chéri's young wife: there is the rivalry between Mme Dalleray and Vinca, between 'Colette' and Hélène Clément in *The Break of Day*, later between Saha the cat and Camille in *La Chatte*. Sometimes the girl wins. Sometimes the young man *returns* to the mother's house. Sometimes the older woman renounces.

All Combray, town and gardens, came out of the
narrator's cup of tea. A sensation, pulling another,
identical, sensation, out of the depths of involuntary
memory, made the childhood which had been forgotten,
that was blank and dry, to unfold, become many-
coloured: like those bits of white paper that the Japanese
dip into water. Colette had much in common with
Proust. She had read him with delight in the Rozven
summers. She knew she was engaged in a similar quest,
and in places will refer herself to Proust in specific terms.
Rainy Moon is shot through with moments of involuntary
memory: 'rainy moon' itself, the phenomenon that gives
its name to the story, is a circle of diffracted light which a
blob in the window pane casts onto the wasted wallpaper
of a forgotten flat. A little round rainbow is thus lit up,
and with it, the forgotten past lights up and fans out.
There is a major difference though between Proust and
Colette. Her access to the many-coloured splendour of
the past came in fits and starts, in separate books and
oblique ways. It occurred inside a continuous, renewed
bond of flesh. She gave birth to a child, she found
fulfilment as a mother, in her writing she resurrected
the women who had mothered her. She housed others,
and that was how she returned to the mother's house.
The movement is not back to your origins from which, in
a chronological sequel, the rest of your past will unroll,
but to and fro between your present and your past, your
future and your present. Every dawn Sido soared to was
a new beginning. A woman's body which has harboured
life, quietly laboured at it, cannot have the same relation
to origins as a man's, unless she does not know what she
knows, is alienated from herself. Through motherhood,
women give birth the way they were themselves given
birth. Flesh passes on. The return to the mother, which is
the figure which underlies much of Colette's work from

La Maison de Claudine onwards, is a movement of progress. The closer Colette gets to Sido, the more she becomes like her mother, the more she begets her own mother through writing, the closer she gets to the heart of life: the centre of the rose.

It is a womanly knowledge. But some men have sensed it. Why else would Dante, at the end of his *Paradiso*, arrived at the innermost circle, the heart of fire of the rose, have Saint Bernard recite a hymn to the Queen of Heaven: 'figlia del tuo figlio' – 'daughter of your own son'?

Colette's work takes place inside the domestic circle: *and* the domestic circle assumes mythical dimensions, becomes as large as the world.

There is on the forum in Rome a black stone, *lapis nigra*. They say that the Romans called it 'umbilicus mundi', the navel of the world. So there was the centre, there in Rome, where a mythical she-wolf had fed the foundling founding twins, Romulus and Remus. I remember being moved by that stone, the thought that for centuries millions of people had been, politically, imaginatively, made to feel centred by it. Why 'umbilicus' though? Is the navel, through which the umbilical cord connected the baby to the womb, at the centre of the body? Strange that it should be a scar, the trace of a bond we had with the submarine world we've lost. *Lapis nigra*, black because its origin is as obscure as the nature of the mother to which it was bound? Is the she-wolf the mythical mother? Two founding twins, Romulus and Remus, sucking the four tits of the she-wolf. Colette had no twin, though Claudine burdened her for long, and her mother's father's daughter. But like da Vinci, she had two mothers, repeatedly: two pairs of teats. Four cardinal points...

In the same period, 'reclined semi-laterally... in the

attitude of Gea-Tellus, fulfilled, recumbent, big with seed', Molly Bloom lies. Her monologue, Joyce tells us,[4] 'turns like the huge earthball slowly, surely evenly, round and round spinning, its four cardinal points being the female breasts, arse, womb and cunt ...' Is there any need to comment on the huge difference between Colette's and Joyce's versions of the four cardinal points? The fertility of Joyce's 'Gea-Tellus' depends on her eternal 'Sleeping Beauty' position, eternally spinning . The still centre of a turning world. Colette's mother-goddess figure, Demeter or Ceres, is the ever-active, mobile, energizing, beneficent mistress of seasons and *knower* of weathers and her children's secrets. Sido's 'rose of the winds' is a new *lapis nigra*. Wonderfully though, Sido never loses an inch of her modest and quizzical humanity. But the concentric circles of significance that expand from her busy thimble are boundless.

Part III
The Recreated Bond

Chapter Eight

The Mother Tongue

' "Beauty", my mother would call me, and "Jewel-of-pure-gold" ' (*Sido*: 147). It took Colette fifty years to return to the kingdom of those names: when having 'become' Colette, the father who had been so beloved of the mother, she grew closer and closer to the mother, the profusion, and confusion of hierarchies, that was Sido's tongue. If Sido had been Adam in the earthly Paradise, naming the creatures, the world of language would have gone differently – and History with it.

'Jewel-of-pure-gold'. The peacock opens its tail/tale of motherly magic. The mother's tongue is like fairy-land. When she speaks, gold and jewels drop from it. Love, dearness. The daughter's worth is absolute. She is her mother's 'masterpiece'. She needs no further reassurance, no further confirmation of her identity. She is not interested in narcissism: the springs she finds taste of the stem of hyacinths, they are close to narcissi, she wants to drink and taste, she is not interested in reflexions and echoes. She is undivided. The mother has

135

told her she was beautiful. The mother's gaze and words of love are all the mirroring she needs.

Sido. Do-re-mi-fa-sol-la-*si-do*. Gabri/elle. *Cabri*: kid. Little Gabri, she/Cabri. -Elle, -ette, -ine. Gabrielle, Colette, Claudine. Diminutives, all feminine. The family punning and nicknames evoke music, and animals. The world of endearments, pet-names, which goes into those strange titles I started from, *Minne, Chéri, Gigi*, is there from the start. The family linguistic habits deny the hierarchies that normally exist between the human and the animal world, as their household does, and Colette's will: she kept cohorts of dogs, cats, a squirrel, a panther, birds... Humans are ennobled by being given animal names. 'Minet-Chéri' means darling kitten, darling puss. There are no louche or jokey connotations, but there *is* love for the precious fur, the long hair of the two daughters that it takes Sido hours to brush every day. 'Ma Toutoune', 'my doggy', is the greatest word of love the sisters in *Le Toutounier* can speak, and they have a code, half-childish, half-animal, for talking to each other. Conversely, animals often have names which are nobler than human names. Saha the cat (*La Chatte*) sounds, and is, more regal and adult than either of the two humans who act out their subtle love and hate through her. And she is more truly female than Alain's bride with the androgynous name: Camille (which is also the name of the lady-in-white in *The Ripening Seed*). *Creatures Great and Small* is filled with wonderfully differentiated and personable beasts. Animals in Colette often understand better, are more dignified, than the humans. The cat of *Chance Acquaintances* acts as a kind of '*cardo*', or axis. She enables her mistress to live through the less palatable side of her curiosity, her willingness to participate in human foibles and lies, without quite losing herself. In *Bella-Vista* the dog Pati-Pati responds to

more modulations, and has a surer sense of people, than
any of the characters. It is not a bit sentimental. Pati-Pati
is 'just' a dog, she discovers or reveals nothing, saves
nobody. But she is thrown into ecstasies of delight when
her 'mother' calls her Pati-Pati-Pati. She knows that
duplication can be a sign of tenderness. Petit-Petit, petit
papa, papa. Toutoune. 'Parti-parti', in baby language,
She reacts with bristling hostility to the the strange
welcome the male inmate of the hotel, M. Daste, gives
her: 'huisipisi'. It is the sound that night-birds make, M.
Daste explains. To perceive how alarming the sound and
its use as a signal are, before the full 'méchanceté' of M.
Daste has been revealed, the reader has to listen, sound
the sound, trust to his/her sense of hearing, like Pati-
Pati. The reader has to be unlike Mme Ruby, the
American lady who is co-manager of the hotel, and who
has never mastered the subtleties of French. Her only
verb, and tense, for 'to be' and 'to have', is 'is': 'est'. 'You
is . . .' Mme Ruby's inability to modulate meaning by
means of grammar is as sure an indication of her
shortcomings, her lack of consideration and self-control,
as Pati-Pati's 'ear' (in the musical sense) shows the kind
of quality Colette as narrator attempts to establish in
that 'odd' story concerned with 'the perverse', interferences between genders, and intercourse between
humans and animals.

It is right to speak of modulation, the vibration of
words. Colette was a good pianist, her brother Léo a
professional. She gloried in having been able to
reproduce on the piano, and sing, a tune which she had
just heard with Debussy, and which Debussy could not
recollect. He looked at M. Willy's country-wife like never
before, and said gently, 'Welcome . . .'.

The register of noises which music can make, that
animals make and that humans in their turn make to

communicate with animals, that mothers like Sido make to express their love for their young, are a major world of sounds in Colette, and one that isn't in the least regarded as undignified. The 'semiotic' occupies in her work a position in relation to the 'symbolic' that modifies the patterns so ingeniously and provocatively described by Julia Kristéva.

She describes the 'semiotic' as having to do with 'archaisms', 'instinctual and maternal'. 'Semiotic processes prepare the future speaker for entrance into meaning and signification (the symbolic)':

> But the symbolic (i.e. language as nomination, sign and syntax) constitutes itself only by breaking with this anteriority, which is retrieved as 'signifier', 'primary processes', displacement and condensation, metaphor and metonymy, rhetorical figures – but which always remains subordinate – subjacent to the principal function of naming – predicating. Language as symbolic function constitutes itself at the cost of repressing instinctual drive and continuous relation to the mother.[1]

She does go on to say that the 'subject of poetic language' does reactivate this repressed instinctual element, and that, since society is established on 'language as communicative code and women as exchange objects', poetic language, by breaking the prohibition of incest (= reactivating the 'maternal' drive), is in a manner of a way 'the *equivalent of incest*'. She invokes as support Artaud, Joyce at the end of *Finnegans Wake*, Céline taking as pseudonym his grandmother's first name; and Sade: 'Unless he becomes his mother's lover from the day she has brought him into the world, let him not bother to write.' And she does evoke, with supple resourcefulness, the variety of positions which the poetic subject can assume, thus caught between the semiotic, maternal, 'incestuous' drive, and the paternal, symbolic, *necessarily sacrificial* function.

Of course, you could say that in so far as the 'semiotic' and the 'symbolic' that Kristéva defines are *both* at work in language, and as the 'poetic subject' is described as feeling strongly the pull towards incest, then this is true of Colette too. Indeed, you could interestingly confront the names 'Colette' and 'Céline', an almost perfect criss-cross. But it does not make all that much sense to talk of the 'prohibition of incest' and of the 'instinctual' drive towards the mother in somebody who went for incest, imaginatively and in life, so repeatedly and so conscious-ly as Colette. Renaud calls Claudine 'my darling child', 'mon enfant chérie', Maxime echoes him, calling Renée 'my darling child' and, as we have seen, there are Missy and Bertrand and my father's daughter and . . . The other thing is that, talking about incest in that way privileges the taboo and the 'sexual' element at the expense of the motherly (or sisterly, brotherly, paternal) love: of what you could call legitimate, multiple, physical, family tenderness. In *Nous, Clytemnestre*,[2] Séverine Auffret shows with eloquence how our culture represses loving between mothers and children, especially mothers and daughters. The Colette family did not, and Sido's way of naming has the effect of bringing the semiotic into the symbolic, of suppressing that war within the poetic subject that founded such conflicts and violence in the writers Kristéva discusses – Sade, Artaud, Céline, Mallarmé. Sido called Gabri 'Minet-Chéri' even when she was a grown woman, she wrote giving her news of 'ta Minne', the cat Colette had given her to keep. The common denominator between Minet-Chéri' and her Minne was that each was dearly beloved of a mother, therefore remarkable and precious. 'Chéri' can become a noun, a name, somebody's only name. Love here is all of a piece, as stable as gold, through and through: 'Jewel of pure gold'. Also a physical bond, the 'furriness' that is so sweet to stroke, also links the daughter and her cat. It is as if a naturally punning babble of love continued into adulthood.

But it's not just sounds that speak, associations that are at work: a quite elaborate system of meanings enables the mother, who disapproves of marriage, of the exchange of women, to gather inside the house of her love creatures that are normally subject to other types of relations. We have seen how it subverts 'normal' oppositions, the one and the two, the One and the Other, absence/presence, animal/human, child/adult. Difference is no longer the absolute corner-stone. The 'toutounier', literally the kennel, the doggy nest, is the huge sofa on which the three-sisters-that-are-four[3] of *Duo* and *Le Toutounier* have grown up, huddled and slept together. It is a bond of physicality between them, a matrix with its own imaginary language, like Gondal, the matrix and imaginary land of the twice-twinned Brontë children. It is not childish, neither a place nor a language to be left behind for the sake of more mature things, but a haven, a hearth that regenerates, where the wounded sisters, mourning or at bay, can come and touch something like mother-earth, and each other. They sleep in each other's arms, front to back, they share their underwear, their make-up, their poverty or their windfalls, their tenderness: what sense would it make to talk of incest, or homosexuality? From their sturdy sofa they sally forth into the world again, more world-wise and brave than most. One, maternal, world, is not what has to be chosen or broken back into at the expense of another, paternal one. They are part and parcel of each other, like the white and yolk of an egg – but an egg engendered out of no violation, holding no knowledge of burnt roofs or broken towers, however great the attraction of a fine blaze or the pain of a broken heart may be – for Captain Colette, who knew real fire and had had a wing broken, had been too much of man to want to prove anything at his loved ones' expense.

Early on in *My Mother's House*, little Colette is described as relishing the sound of unknown words. She delights in 'presbytery', hurling it at people as an insult from the top of the garden wall. It's the 'semiotic' all right: the child revels in the sound, she vents aggression through it, not knowing what it 'means'. The signifier functions independently from the signified, carrying 'archaic' drives.

There is comparable word-play in Colette's contemporaries: in Joyce's *Portrait of The Artist as a Young Man*, for instance. The child, who has caught a fever from being thrown into mud by bullies, plays with the word 'kiss'. His mother has kissed him goodnight just as the sickness was coming on. The word is sticky, it has to do with mud, disgust. It turns into the reverse of the mother's goodnight kiss in Proust's *Combray*, where it is highly-charged, signals the narrator's dependence upon what eludes his grasp. In Proust it is a 'viatique', a holy communion, to which impending night, the mother's absence, death, imparts desperation. The experience lays the foundation for the narrator's future relation to love. Perhaps for Stephen Dedalus also, the mother's kiss and the peculiar relation to the mother's body that the sickness gives it, is already establishing the ground for his later relations to women. But what is paramount in the Joyce passage is the way in which the sound 'kiss' leaves the concept 'kiss' and associates with sensations felt to be the tactile equivalent of the sound. Nausea mutates from the moment in the ditch and the ensuing fever to a word which, culturally, both denotes and connotes what is most 'sacred' and enjoyable: the mother's kiss.

Colette's use of 'presbytery' is closer to Joyce than to Proust. The sound is allowed to range freely in association with basic drives, outside the respectable, religious connotations of the word as well as its meaning. Yet there is a difference. The play of sounds for her is pure delight: 'Presbytère': learned, pompous, a grown-up thing to be mocked. *Clystère, presbyte, phalanstère. Oh ma chère.* It's rather like Captain Haddock's register of insults in *Tintin*. You can play with it if you do so by ear. The child is not trying to rise to a world of wisdom, of poetry, as Stephen will when, as an adolescent, he becomes enamoured with language. Her speech instead is on its way to Gondal. It is wild, unsociable, a private code. She is trying to create in language a mode of being that is an alternative to the adult world, and yet that turns its own tools against it. 'Presbytère' descends, as an insult, upon the adults to be chastised.

In a wonderful late story, 'The Sick Child', the child *rides* the sounds of words to escape from the 'real' world of grown-ups and illness that he inhabits. He looks at an 'immmmmense' silver paper-cutter, and its multiplied 'm's give him wings, enable him to ride it. He plays with the glorious 'doré', golden name of the servant, 'Mandore', he feels drawn to the 'golden' thing that goes by the name of *'mort'*, death. It holds both 'or', gold, and 'm'. Yet all the 'm's of his 'babble', sound the base-drum of the word for love, the word for pleasure, the 'mmmm' that beats softly four times in the name he gives his mother: 'Madame Maman'. Sounds that human bodies make or that their mouths articulate are never repulsive in Colette: from Charlotte's 'roucoulade', the cooing song that pleasure draws from her or that she modulates as a homage to her young lover, in *The Pure and the Impure*,

to Chéri's perception of a couple of lovers on a bench in
the Bois de Boulogne, at night, on his return from war.
There comes from them

> the rustle of crushed clothes and smothered endearments.
> Chéri listened for an instant to the clasped bodies and
> invisible lips, a sound like the ripple of a ship's prow cleaving
> calm waters.
>
> 'The man's a soldier,' he noticed. 'I've just heard him
> unbuckle his belt.' (*L of Ch*: 140)

The *precision* of Chéri's listening in the dark is pure
Colette. For even as a child, she played with words *astride*
the garden wall: that is, still within the safety of the
mother's house, but aware of the power of words on the
world outside and keen to master that power. As a
writer, she will work with several dictionaries, passionate in her quest of 'le mot juste'. Though her father
provided the books, the writing implements, the dream
of writing, it was Sido who passionately insisted on
'predicates and names', what is supposed to pertain to
the 'symbolic': on the specificity of plants, insects.
Colette's admiration will go more and more to people
whose lore is based, like her mother's, on a lived relation
to the things they can name and describe. As to the
woodman of the Fontainebleau forest whom she
describes in *Flore et Pomone*, whose knowledge of herbs
and trees and flowers and beasts puts her to shame. For
language that attempts to render the identity of things
does not thrive at the expense of things. The writer who
can produce such language produces actual nurture
without robbing life. That is presumably why *Flore et
Pomone* ends with a kind of hymn in which Colette
expresses the wish that her writing were a *loam* in which
things could find nourishment. An image that is a far cry

from the customary 'seed and harvest' images that so many writers use. Where, pray, in loam, are the semiotic and the symbolic? As for the child Sartre portrays himself as having been, in *Words*, his relation to the Dictionary was the reverse of Colette's: he thought that the 'Ideas', words like 'trees', were in the *Larousse*; and the fallen things, trees, in the Luxembourg gardens.

No such upstairs-downstairs for Colette.

It is fortunate that the linguistic attitudes Colette had imbibed from her mother were in effect encouraged and cross-fertilized by the literary milieu – the aftermath of Symbolism – in which Willy made her live. Willy breathed 'calembours', he doated on puns, on the instability of words in language. Or rather, on the play of permutations. Ubu's 'merdre' is exemplary. Add one letter and you change everything. The word becomes almost acceptable on stage, the extra 'r' somehow makes it even more of a swear-word, more 'shit-like'; it also makes it odd, makes it suggest other words, 'mettre', 'mère'. Colette is engaged in her own game of verbal musical chairs in the names of her partners in life. 'Missy' is rather like 'Willy', the 'M' a 'W' upside down. Missy herself put her name in the mirror when she mimed in *Rêve d'Egypte* under the pseudonym 'Yssim'. Reflect your name and it becomes Eastern. 'Sidi', 'Master' in Arabic, is the nickname of Colette's next partner, Henry de Jouvenel. I, y, i. Willy, Missy, Sidi. Since 'Sidi' means 'Master', Colette is out of the androgynous fold, then? Ah, but Sidi sounds very like Sido. Was Sido really a master then, or does Sidi remind Colette of her mother? 'Missy' suggests 'little Miss', but also young mistress, bossy boots. In *Creatures Great and Small*, 'la Shah', the lord, is a Persian cat that was bought as a tom, named accordingly: but it turns out to be a she-cat, which in no way diminishes its lordly ways. It

probably inspired the *Russian*-sounding name of aristocratic Saha. Maguerite Moréno lovingly called Colette
'Loleth', an Eastern-sounding name. The women's love-
language reclaims that world of the Orient where the
Romantic imagination had placed its dream of the
'houri'. As for brother Léo – did he suggest to Colette the
name of Léa?

The mutations are spread throughout Colette's entire
work and not just with people's names. It's not quite
metaphor; not quite metonymy. But it strikes me that it
takes an extraordinarily *sane* identity to take such
continued relish in such permutations. Yet again Colette
does not fit the defined categories. The subconscious is
at work (in the pursuit of the mother's name, echoes of
her name), but the ego knows it well, and plays with its
knowledge. Dolphins in the sea. But then, we've seen
that Colette had precious little superego: the world of
taboos inspiring so little awe, is there any wonder that
the totems should be so unstable, in and out of
something like a liquid element, alive. Yes, like dolphins
in the sea.

Or bulbs and chrysalis in a rich loam.

Chapter Nine

Currencies

The mother's letters

In *Remembrance of Things Past*, Mme de Sévigné, famous for the letters she wrote her daughter, is the grandmother's favourite author. The tender bond between herself and her daughter, the narrator's mother, is suggested through the love of Mme de Sévigné for her daughter, What if Mme Proust had had a daughter instead of a son? What would a 'Marcelle' have been?

There is a peculiar fascination in western culture for the letters women write.[1] From Vermeer to Mme Vigée-Lebrun and many more, painters have depicted women writing or receiving letters. Somehow you always know that it is a letter, *not a book*, that is being penned, folded, perused. Generally, you also know that it is a love-letter. Perhaps because the painting makes you speculate amorously about the woman, as though the letter she was reading, which may be seducing her or recalling seduction to her, made her accessible to you. The letter

gives you entry into the woman's 'interiority', it makes
you guess what she is looking so deep or so cunning
about. Most such paintings are by men, and they are
meant to be seen, perused, by men. The woman who is
thus represented is almost a letter herself, a love-letter
that is being sent by one man to others. By means of the
letter, the woman circulates: as Lacan argues that
femininity does. Like the letter in Poe's story, femininity
is a 'purloined letter'.

Claudine Hermann has pursued this theme. *Les Voleuses
de langue*[2] shows how, in a number of texts (ranging from
the seventeenth to the twentieth century), analogies are
created or unconsciously established between women
and letters. Both are blank, messages are inscribed upon
them by men, who stamp them with the stamp of
ownership. In Barbey d'Aurevilly's *Les Diaboliques*, the
analogy is crude between the mistress who is *sealed* by her
infuriated lover's red-hot sword, and the red wax seal on
the love-letter she was reading as he came into the room.

But when, as with Mme de Sévigné, the mother writes
to her daughter, the writing is of quite another kind. She
perpetuates the loving bond between them. Her letters
make both the sender and the addressee participants in a
live, reciprocal relationship, instead of objects of exchange. It is to exploring the creative implications of that
bond that *The Break of Day* is dedicated. It opens,
significantly, with a letter from Sido refusing an
invitation from Colette's new husband, Henry de
Jouvenel. She longs to see her daughter, but she will not
come, she says. She is waiting for the rare and short-
lived blossoming of her pink cactus. In real life, Sido *had*
come. What the 'fictitious' letter signifies is Sido's
refusal of the circulation of women: 'No, I will not give
you my daughter, I will not be a party to that type of
exchange. The flowering of my cactus is a greater *event*

than what the world regards as a major event: marriage.'
Through Sido, Colette rewrites her own history as well
as her own fiction: since *The Shackle*, drawn out of the
affair with Jouvenel, leaves Renée intent upon love only,
summoning the one, the only being that mattered:
'Jean!'. J, like Jouvenel.

The Break of Day is an extraordinary novel, if that is the
word for it. Extracts from Sido's letters to Colette
alternate with an episode in the narrator's, 'Colette's',
life. She is spending the summer at her Saint-Tropez
house, La Treille Muscate. A young neighbour, Vial,
often calls. Colette is told by a young friend, Hélène
Clément, that Vial is in love with her, Colette, and that
this is what prevents him from taking heed of Hélène's
own love for him. Hélène asks Colette to send Vial
packing, so she can have a chance. This Colette does, for
complicated reasons among which the desire to learn to
renounce, as Sido knew, plays a part. But not before she
has watched Vial's love for her blaze through the night
until dawn, as Sido, in a letter that I have already
mentioned and that is quoted, watched her neighbour's
barn blaze from her window at dawn. The mother's
letters, that is, serve to adumbrate the promise of a
better, older, more contemplative self. They help the
narrator enact her rite of passage, *not into death*, but into
age: not as a defeat, or the loss of youth and beauty, but
as a path towards something higher, however humble.
Higher, like the sky towards which the lark which Sido
watched, rose every morning. The dawn with which the
book ends is the *birth* of a new day. *La Naissance du jour*, not
'the *break* of day', which sounds brittle and violent.
Through her letters, her growth of influence in her
daughter's life, Sido gives birth to her daughter again.
Advancing in age, Colette moves closer to the age her
mother was when she admired and cherished her best,

when she had moved far beyond the 'gay little vampire' that exhausted the maternal heart. Writing, Colette develops the talent her mother wanted to foster: 'You have a real talent as a writer, Minet-Chéri.' She creates her own mother.[3] She is being her mother's daughter, the daughter of a woman who taught her to speak and wrote such splendid letters. 'Is it not clear which of us is the better writer?', Colette asks, meaning Sido is. Even the last letter from Sido is not just the ultimate lesson in learning 'the supreme elegance of knowing how to diminish'. It is a *love-letter*, already *beyond* language, and it points the way to experimental writing:

> No doubt my mother wrote that last letter to assure me that she no longer felt any obligation to use our language. Two pencilled sheets have on them nothing more than apparently joyful signs, arrows emerging from an embryo word, little rays, 'yes, yes' together, and a single 'she danced', very clear. Lower down she had written 'my treasure' – her name for me when our separations had lasted a long time and she was longing to see me again. But this time I feel a scruple in claiming for myself so burning a word. It has a place among strokes, swallow-like interweavings, plant-like convolutions – all messages from a hand that was trying to transmit to me a new alphabet or the sketch of some ground-plan envisaged at dawn under rays that would never attain the sad zenith. So that instead of a confused delirium, I see in that letter one of those haunted landscapes where, to puzzle you, a face lies hidden among the leaves, an arm in the fork of a tree, a body under a cluster of rock. (*B of D*: 142)

Letters and the circulation of women

The fate of the letter in western fiction is puzzling. The

eighteenth century is a period in which women, following in the seventeenth-century tradition of Mme de Sévigné, wrote wonderful letters: like Mme du Deffand or Melle de Lespinasse, who kept *salons* where famous writers came, the Encyclopaedists, foreigners like Walpole. The ladies themselves do not seem to have written books, certainly not as many as their seventeenth-century predecessors. But they wrote letters, which have survived as 'Literature', like Mme de Sévigné. Somehow there was licence to 'pen' great prose when it had a private addressee, and was meant neither for a commercial purpose nor a wide audience. The letter stayed inside the domestic circle, or the *salon* circle. It went to and fro between private individuals, it had no public function but it might be read to a select circle of listeners inside the drawing-room.

The epistolary novel grew in that century and out of such letters. In England, Richardson was called to the rescue by local ladies who found that the lad had the knack of turning a pretty phrase. They needed help to write letters, as an illiterate soldier might need the help of a literate sergeant to write home when he is at war. Richardson did so well at writing as if he was a woman that he turned it into a livelihood. He devised a set of fictitious circumstances that required a large number of letters to be written. And there was Pamela, writing to her parents about how yet again she had withstood Mr B's attempt at seduction. Later, there were Clarissa, and Miss Howe. And with them, Lovelace and Bedford. And Julie and Saint-Preux, in Rousseau's *La Nouvelle Héloïse*. And Valmont and La Merteuil, in Laclos's *Les Liaisons dangereuses*. And Werther. And Foscolo's *Le Ultime lettere di Iacopo Ortis*. And . . . and . . . and then, the epistolary novel peters out in the first half of the nineteenth century. Why, is a complicated question. But interestingly, one of

its last offshoots is by Colette's favourite writer with
Proust, Balzac: *The Memoirs of Two Young Brides*. Two
young girls who have been bosom friends at the convent
are recalled by their families to be married. One has to
make do with an arranged marriage to an unexciting
young old man, but motherhood fulfils her. The other
goes for broke, she has two love-matches, but with each,
tragedy strikes. The two women narrate their daily lives
and loves to each other in their letters. The sensible one
is called... Renée. Balzac must have chosen the form
because of its pretended naturalness. How else but by
fictitiously intercepting letters could a man gain entry,
not only into a convent, but into the intimacy of two
young women? For his *Religieuse*, the inside account of
convent life, Diderot already had chosen the form of an
autobiographical letter begging for protection. Colette
will half-imitate that tradition by making Claudine write
her 'diary' of school events.

It seems to me that, as the nineteenth century moves
on and passes into the twentieth, novelists become less
interested in gaining, or pretending to gain, 'natural'
access to their material. Of course, you still find diary-
type narrations, or tales within tales, reported 'oral'
stories. There are Conrad's Marlowe and the governess
in James's *The Turn of the Screw*: but both the sailor's yarn
and the Gothic tale are survivors of another age.
Certainly, neither James in the main, nor Zola, nor
Lawrence, nor Proust when he writes about Swann, nor
Joyce are interested in showing through what channels
they, *as narrators*, have come to know about the intimate
feelings of Bloom or Ursula or Gervaise or Maisie. The
petering out of the epistolary novel is one of the signs of
that loss of interest, which may signal the increasing
isolation of the individual. For when characters tell their
own story, they are speaking of what they have

experienced, and for a particular addressee. When they exchange letters, there is reciprocity, and the 'reader' is individualized and expected to respond. In the light of all this, wild as my speculations may be, it is interesting that the diary form, and the epistolary form, play a major part in Colette's work.

With the exception of *L'Ingénue libertine*, all her works are from the horse's mouth until *Chéri*. The Claudine novels are all 'written', or rather spoken, by Claudine, since her 'paysanne pervertie' gift of the gab is the essence of their charm. *The Vagabond* and *The Shackle* are carried by the spontaneousness of Renée's utterance, *Music-Hall Sidelights* are in the voice of Renée/Colette, *Creatures Great and Small* are either animal dialogues or in a tone that is expressive of the animals themselves. *Mitsou* is a combination of theatre dialogue and epistolary novel. Indeed, letters play a decisive role in the novels. In *Claudine Married* and *The Vagabond*, a letter to the loved man takes over from the 'speaking' character at the end. The discovery of love-letters by a mistress to her husband precipitates Annie's departure. Letters mark the progress of Claudine's withdrawal, in *The Sentimental Retreat*. In *Mitsou*, they show the reverse, a growth in commitment. The subtitle is 'Comment l'esprit vient aux filles', 'How wit comes to girls'. Like Agnès in Molière's *L'Ecole des femmes*, Mitsou, the little music-hall artiste is barely literate. She makes spelling mistakes, feels all funny about writing letters to the blue lieutenant who is at the front and whom she's fallen for. But, as with Agnès and better than with Agnès, love makes her take giant strides. She grows in wit and literacy, but also in great-hearted delicacy as her love blossoms, and she perceives it is not reciprocated, and she accepts this.

From *Chéri* onwards, it is as though Colette had grown in confidence, and decided to move to third-person narrative. She does so as a thorough mistress of the first-person voice, of 'innerness', as well as of the exchange that is in dialogue: she could adapt *Chéri* as well as *The Vagabond* for theatre. But the third person enables her to render all the unspoken intercourse that accompanies dialogue. Her texts convey both the uncensored, almost wild, presence of the body of the protagonists, and the circulation, the speedy, shifting skein of exchanges and perceptions that go on between them. She combines first-person and second-person into a mobile and distinctive third-person. The reader is in, and out. There is plenty that s/he has to guess. Sometimes Colette reminds me of late Henry James, except that it's faster, you see more of the 'outside', know more about the bodies of the protagonists. But there is a similar lack of voyeurism, an interest in intimacy and respect for privacy. It's there in Philippe's 'break' at the hands of the lady-in-white as in all the charged moments in the later novels:

His hostess had risen to serve him, and soon he was sipping, from a small silver shovel, the sugar-sprinkled, anis-flavoured red flesh of the melon.

'Are your relatives enjoying good health, Monsieur Phil?'

He stared up at her in surprise. She looked slightly distraught and did not appear to have heard her own voice. He scooped up a spoon in his cuff and it fell on the carpet with the plaintive tinkle of a small bell.

'Clumsy! Just you wait...'

She caught hold of his wrist with one hand, and with the other she rolled up his sleeve as far as the elbow, keeping a firm grip on his bare arm with her hot hand.

'Let me go!' Phil cried in a piercing tone.

He jerked his arm away so violently that a saucer broke in pieces at his feet. The echo of Vinca's 'Let go!' shrilled through the buzzing in his ears, and he turned to Mme

Dalleray with a glare of questioning fury. She had not moved, and the hand he had cast aside so roughly lay open on her lap like a hollow shell. It took Philippe some little time to weigh up the significance of her motionless attitude. He let his head drop forward, and in front of his eyes passed an incoherent vision of two or three self-images, in which he was either swimming ineluctably through the air, as one flies in dream, or plunging headlong down, as in a dive, at the very moment when the ripples rise up to strike the down-turned face; and then, without enthusiasm, but with deliberate slowness and calculated courage, he put his bare arm back into her open hand. (*RS*: 69)

There is an even heightened complexity of exchange in *The Break of Day*: when for instance Hélène asks Colette to let go of Vial. The first-person narration has in its turn been enriched by previous use of the third-person. The memory of the mother's letter and its quotation add depth to the layers of time that the suspended moment calls up, and articulate the movement between 'inside' and 'outside'. Involuntary memory writes in the mother's hand:

What she still had to say did not pass her lips. She still had to say to me, 'Madam, I believe you are the . . . the friend of Vial, and that is why Vial cannot love me.' I might easily have said it for her, but the moments passed and neither of us made up our mind to speak. Hélène pushed her armchair back a little and the blaze of light caressed her face. I felt sure that in an instant the whole of that youthful planet, with its bare, rounded, moon-like forehead and cheeks, was going to crack up, rent by an earthquake of sobs. The white down round her mouth, as a rule scarcely visible, was beaded with a dew of emotion. Hélène wiped her temples with the end of her striped scarf. A passionate desire to be sincere, and the odour of an irritated blonde, emanated from her, although she kept silent with all her might. She implored me to understand, not to force her to speak; but I suddenly stopped troubling about her, in so far as she was **Hélène Clément**. I put her into her niche in the universe, among the spectacles of other days of which I had been the anonymous spectator or the proud begetter. That decent silly creature will never know that I held her worthy to rank in my memory with my tears for my adolescent joys: the shock of my first sight of a dawn of dark fire on an iron-blue peak covered with violet snow; the flower-like unfolding of the crinkled hand of a new-born babe; the echo of a single long note taking wing from the throat of a bird, low at first, then so high that I confused it, at the moment when it broke off, with the gliding of a shooting star; and those flames, my very dear, those dishevelled peonies of flame that the fire shook over your garden. You sat down happily, spoon in hand, *since it was nothing but straw*. (B of D: 74–5)

Letters, money, the female body

Poe's *The Purloined Letter* represents the triangular situation (which the two passages just quoted so clearly rewrite), and the role of the love-letter, in an archetypal way. Queen receives letter. Love-letter one assumes. King must not see it. If King saw it, King would do something terrible, for his wife as his property has been tampered with, or his power has been threatened. We know this through Queen's speed at concealing letter when King enters her Chamber. If third person – Minister – can get hold of letter, he can blackmail Queen. Use letter to get power, or money: 'If you don't do so and so, I'll show your letter to King.' This is what goes on between King, Queen and Cardinal in Dumas' *The Three Musketeers*. Between Lord Dedlock, Lady Dedlock, and Mr Tulkinghorn in Dickens' *Bleak House*. In Balzac's *Ferragus*, the jealous husband steals his wife's letter to the man he suspects of being her lover. The pursuit and suspicion kill her.

It is the man who dies in Colette's *Duo*. She once more rewrites the triangular situation, and the role of the love-letter in it. Michel accidentally comes across a love-letter to his wife Alice. They are happy, in love. Michel is now ravaged by jealousy, his whole life eaten up by what he takes to be a stupendous revelation. Alice keeps assuring him that the affair did not matter: she means it too. Michel wants to know who the lover was, and the revelation that it is his production partner increases the pain: he has nothing against the partner, Alice is the source and focus of the grief. He tells Alice he would not mind so much if it had been 'just physical', the kind of passion men feel. What he cannot bear is that women put so much emotion into their affairs. So Alice, desperate for him to regain some peace, shows him the rest of the correspondence, which proves conclusively that physical passion was all that it was, a flash in the pan. Instead of being relieved, Michel is devastated: he goes out at night and drowns himself in the swollen river at the bottom of the estate.

A number of clichés are subverted: the suggestion that women cannot experience 'just' physical passion – and what does that mean, anyway? – the notion that there is anything to 'know' that would be relevant to the husband. Alice does not feel guilty. In the sequel, *The Toutonier*, she feels excruciating pain at Michel's death, his absence: because she loved him. But she also feels anger at the gratuitousness of his death, his inability to live with a knowledge that to her was no knowledge. She remains outside the triangular situation, there can be no question of blackmail any more than of guilt. Indeed, the third person in *Duo* is not Ambrogio the lover who never appears, except on reported calls on the telephone and snippets of writing, but the servant Maria, who is Michel's old housekeeper and who initially is loyal to him. She guesses what is going on between husband and wife, she herself being frequently beaten by a jealous husband, and she silently enters into a bond of complicity with Alice. Subtle relations between the two women, beyond class boundaries, are substituted for the equation between women and letters, women as objects to be exchanged, possessed, prevented from circulating. There is a currency of human relations, and objects remain objects, creatures creatures: to Michel who is impatient with a bee at the breakfast table, Alice says, 'Can't you see that it's hungry and it's working?' The bee is an example of the values that the text allows. Its relation to things is fuelled by hunger (desire), and it is one of labour. Marx would have approved, however bizarre the coupling of the names Marx and Colette may sound. As always in Colette, the language goes, not for metaphor (though the concision and unexpectedness create the impression of metaphor) but for simile. In the simile, things remain separate. As separate as Maria and the floor she *actively* polishes and develops a rhythm towards, as separate as the surface of the floor and the surface of the river in this famous passage:

> Maria ... was polishing the floor with felt pattens on her feet, her lean brown arms swinging out loosely in a regular rhythm, her goat legs dancing with scissor-like movements. She moved over the polished floor like a water spider over the pewter surface of a pond. (*Duo*: 85)

In metaphor, things tend to become one. To merge. The surface breaks, it's water, you are subsumed by it, you drown. Or you become trapped by a reflexion. It is striking here that Maria remains *on the surface*, and that surface is pewter, it does not reflect. Alice too remains on the surface. Both women are survivors, they have a strong, sensuous relation to the world. The illusion of depth in *Duo* is the fascination for death. Seeing more to a situation than there is, allowing his imagination of an event to engulf him, leads Michel to drowning. At the end of the novel, he walks into the swollen river whose mud had remained caked on the surface of the polished floor in the opening scene.

> He walked briskly down the slope, crossed the thicket where it was still dark and met the river as it lapped silently against the fence, its water slow-moving and heavy with iron-red mud. (*Duo*: 131).

The river is almost solid, like a beast, it's almost as if it didn't want to be drowned into.

Julie de Carneilhan is divorced from D'Espivant, whom she still loves. She is broke, middle-aged, lives in a small flat, but is also as handsome and stylish as ever. She is suddenly summoned to D'Espivant's bedside: he has had a heart attack. He is now married to a wealthy woman who keeps him short. He has expensive tastes, wishes for a degree of freedom, still longs for Julie, perhaps? He needs a million francs to gain some elbow-room. Julie might help, and who knows what might not happen, then? When he first married Julie, she had diamonds from her first husband. They had sold them for a million francs and spent the money together, but D'Espivant in his pride had given Julie a note stating that he owed her a million francs. If Julie were to produce the note, threaten to sue, then D'Espivant's jealous rich wife would pay: Julie and D'Espivant could split the sum. Julie has destroyed the note. However, she is tempted, half-seduced. She agrees to letting D'Espivant claim to Marianne, his wife, that the note exists, that Julie is threatening. Julie waits for a letter from D'Espivant, telling her that now they have the money, they can start all over again. She is waiting for a love-letter, which her own pretended blackmail should have gained her. Instead, she gets a visit from Marianne. An extraordinary encounter, in which rivalry, jealousy, fighting with all the weapons of their own good looks, elegant clothes, bind the two women into a state of mutual knowledge and appreciation, both of each other's beauty, and of the value of the man they are fighting for.

After Marianne's departure, Julie finds that a letter has been left. A fat envelope. Yet from the weight Julie knows. Several layers of paper wrap up a hundred thousand francs. D'Espivant has sent her 10 per cent, as if she had been his agent, and that was her commission, Julie thinks. And not a word of love with it. Money instead of love, and on top of it she's been robbed (the diamonds had been hers, after all) as Marianne has been robbed, and both women have been used to rob each other:

> The top envelope enclosed another in which, wrapped in several thicknesses of tissue paper was a bundle of blue and pinkish notes that finally emerged, pinned together in trusses of ten, brand new, and smelling faintly of tallow. 'Is that all? Why, there are only a hundred thousand francs, and not a word. Not even an impertinent little "Thank you", – not even the sort of joke a cheerful swindler might scribble, to make me laugh? (*J de C*: 178)

There is a memory of Jouvenel here – after his divorce from Colette he had married a very wealthy woman, whose money could help his political career. No doubt, in earlier years, he had helped Colette spend her literary earnings. The initials of Julie de Carneilhan, J de C, reverse those of Colette de Jouvenel, C de J, and that must be a kind of signature. But there is also a memory of Willy. Not just because, in the days of his separation from Colette, he had tried to inveigle Colette into a *coup* similar to D'Espivant's; but because the equation between writing and money was one which he had bottle-fed to his young wife. In *Julie de Carneilhan*, the envelope which should contain a love-letter contains money instead. Prostitution, and with it all the operations that make women into exchangeable, profit-making goods, are embryonically there.

But it does not work that way. Julie's very way of looking at, and touching the banknotes, shows it. She is interested in their colour, the pink and blue, the smell, the feel of the paper, what kind it is. She no more thought that the diamonds represented her worth to her first husband, than that they were hers rather than D'Espivant's, when it came to spending their value. It is interesting that Colette should have chosen an aristocratic heroine, and a ruined one at that, who ends up going to live with her brother in the derelict family castle, as Colette might have dreamed of returning with brother Léo to the Saint-Sauveur house. For the aristocrat voices the same contempt for, and carelessness towards, money, as the music-hall artistes had taught Colette in earlier years. Years which had helped Colette cleanse her body from louche relations with money. And gain the perception that money is paper is money is diamonds is money is paper: but not people. People get money, people earn money, people spend money. There are active verbs, and the rich array of the senses, between people and money.

Colette had earned a living with her body. Miming,

half-naked, working hard at it, like the bee of *Duo*. She had not been a courtesan, but sometimes she must have come close to being 'kept' by Missy, though neither Missy nor herself perceived the relation in those terms. She had lived in a world of women who made money by means of their looks and charm and know-how – on-stage or off-stage. Who, however, had a relation to money of a quite independent character. Not a single one of Colette's 'mondaines' or 'demi-mondaines' is affected as a person by her supposed bondage to cash. Jadin is cross when Renée laughs at her appreciation of the quality of the flowers she's been given by 'the chap' she 'did a bunk with the other day':

> She turns quite red under her powder and takes offence:
>   'What is it? P'raps you don't believe he was a gentleman? All right, ask Canut, the stage-setter, to let you see what I brought back in the way of brass, last night when you'd just gone!
>   'How much?'
>   'Sixteen hundred francs, dearie! Canut saw them, it isn't a yarn!' Do I look sufficiently impressed? I fear not.
>   'And what are you going to do with it, Jadin?'
>   She plucks unconcernedly at the threads hanging from her old blue and white dress: 'Don't suppose there'll be any for savings. I stood the stage-hands a round of drinks. And then I lent – as she calls it – fifty francs to Myriame to pay for her coat. And the girls keep asking one after the other and saying they haven't got a bean. I really don't know!'
> (V: 45–6)

Jadin's milieu is exactly Nana's. But neither the determinism nor the brutality that make Nana a bundle of lusts and the offspring of corruption, a golden fly on the turd of Capital, a money-sucker preying upon money, have any relevance to Colette. Sure, life is hard,

women need money, the fate of Jadin, Gribiche or
Lucette is cruel: the women are exposed to consumption
(which Jadin is dying of: Sido endlessly worried about
her daughter catching colds on stage), to the hazards of
backstreet abortions, to the caprices of sadistic rich
lovers and the foolishness of the besotted ones. Yet they
are never reducible to the material odds of their lives.
Colette knew plenty about those odds, and more at first
hand than Zola: she spent six years at least in the
milieu. 'These men do not know what they're talking
about,' Sido had told Gabri when she'd found her fainting
from the horror of a birth scene in Zola. Perhaps Colette
can also be trusted better than Zola in her account of the
Nanas of this world.

Mitsou is kept by a 'Monsieur Bien', a Respectable
Gentleman. That seems to her a perfectly adequate
arrangement until she falls in love with the Blue
Lieutenant. Her bedroom furniture is in bad taste, the
dream of a poor girl who has admired prize bourgeois
pieces in her childhood and decided to have them all.
Mitsou is a bit like Crevel in Balzac's *La Cousine Bette*.
Crevel has his *salon* designed by the now old-fashioned
and vulgar architect Grindot, whose productions he's
admired in his master's apartments when he was an
apprentice-perfumier. But Mitsou is capable of total
disinterestedness. Like Jadin, she's prepared to lose every
penny she's been given by her rich lover. Léa, another
and grander courtesan, is a wonderful housekeeper.
When she staggers under the full blast of her passion for
Chéri, whom she knows age will force her to lose, feeling
ill, so acute is the pain, she decides to tidy up and re-line
her drawers. That'll keep her sane. After realizing she's
been sent money instead of a love-letter, Julie de
Carneilhan washes up, then polishes her riding-boots,
soldiering on through the night and through despair

thanks to competent domestic gestures. Instead of being reduced to commodities, these women who do use their bodies as currency according to merchant ethics, are free and fresh in relation to the money they earn and the objects they own. They do not mix business with pleasure. Lucette, in *Chance Acquaintances*, keeps her relation with her lover quite distinct from those with the wealthy gents who provide the dough. And she is right. For when it comes to actual worth, the Lucettes and Luigis of this world, ordinary as they may be, are found to have greater 'value' than those who pay for their services. Hearing of Lucette's death from blood-poisoning, the result of a terrible wound a previous wealthy gent with sadistic leanings inflicted upon her, the narrator, whose sympathies have ebbed and flowed between Gérard Haume, whose passion for the likes of Lucette moved her, Antoinette his wife, whose tactful jealousy she respected, and happy-go-lucky, undistinguished Lucette, falls firmly on the side of Lucette:

> ... I would have liked to have shouted: 'She died in the arms of her kind-hearted tough, who was waiting for her each time she came back from the ends of the earth, in a galleon, a car, a cart, or bare-foot, and gashed to the bone. A kind, humble tough, a real lover, capable of facing the death of a vagrant mistress and announcing it without fuss, and of never getting over it. Dear Antoinette and sensitive Gérard, I'll try not to think too much of this couple when you are close at hand in case I should find the pair of you a bit colourless by comparison... (*Ch. Acq.*: 76)

Balzac, who believed that women were a species apart, not reducible to any of the classifiable male species, had also sensed something like Colette when he had portrayed the girl with the golden eyes. She may symbolize gold to those who desire her, wish to possess her exclusively, hoard her or, on the contrary, want to make her current. All she cares about is love. She has no normative notions of property. To the man who has seduced her away from her woman lover, and who won't run away with her because, he says, he has not got enough money to keep her, she proposes to take the gold that is in her lover's house. We can't, it would be stealing, the young man replies. You've taken me, she says: why not the gold? She is both in and out of Capital. In, because she is beautiful, poor, and needs to live. Out, because she does not think herself reducible to her exchange value. Neither do Colette's 'filles de joie'.

And so, her gigolos and courtesans never are what you might expect. She protested against Chéri being called a gigolo. 'Diabolo' might be more appropriate, she argued, for Chéri is dark, demonic, eerily gifted for love. And frail, like beings who come from another, more absolute, world. A gigolo, Chéri? He's rich. His mother has made a lot of money as a courtesan. His wife is heiress to a large fortune accumulated by the same means by her mother. Both mothers in fact arrange a marriage as if it were an arch-bourgeois marriage – which it is: the alliance of two well-managed and now respectable fortunes. Like all money that looks as if it's here to stay. The stock exchange has no mysteries for these ex-courtesans, initially as good with frills and graces as Laura Ashley was with pencil and cloth. Acute business sense made the rest. Chéri's and Edmée's money has been laundered by good management and, quite simply, the fact that gold and pleasure rule the Paris of pre-1914 as they did the July Monarchy in Balzac's day. The noble family in *Sarrasine* are heirs to a courtesan, a castratum who successfully traded on his voice and good looks in the Republic of Venice. Vautrin the convict constructs Lucien de Rubempré's fortune out of the 'million' he makes Esther the courtesan pump out of Nucingen the banker, so that Lucien can marry aristocratic Clothilde de Grandlieu. The context is more surprising in Colette than in Balzac, for she throws you in at the deep end, registers no apparent awareness of how the world's value, or hypocrisy, would normally function. But Léa's passion for Chéri, Chéri's for Léa, is worth what it is, quite independently of the money they both use and take for granted: just about everything. Just about. If Chéri dies, Léa survives.

On the other hand, D'Espivant, who is 'the best' – aristocratic, socially distinguished, surrounded by luxury, and distinctly 'virile' – a powerful figure, a man irresistible to women, a 'master' – does behave as a gigolo. He has gleefully eaten his first wife's 'million'. He now gets a second million from his second wife by playing upon his first wife's passion for him so she'll help him blackmail his second wife. The man is everything the world respects: at the centre of the social stage, a husband and a gentleman. But he behaves like Maxime de Trailles, the dandy who ruins his mistress and gets her to ruin her family, in Balzac. In Balzac it is the dandy, the bachelor, the threat upon the sacred institution of marriage, who is the gigolo. In Colette, the very pillar and foundation of marriage, the husband-and-father-and-Sidi, is behaving like a gigolo. Normative social and moral values are being redistributed.

This means that nothing can be taken for granted. You have to see each thing, each person, for what they are. Nothing is cliché, nothing is given. Objects, for instance, do not bear out the customary gender distinctions. Jewellery is not women's specific province. Pearls are particularly interesting in Colette. They register a specifically feminine status in many ways. A lot of her female characters own and wear pearls, the craft of pearl-stringing – and all its associations – and the need to have one's pearl necklace restrung every year are part and parcel of life: a history of this is evoked in the story, *The Photographer's Lady*. The quality of the pearls, the way you wear them, are not just a sign a wealth, but can be a declaration of intent. Thus when Marianne visits Julie, Julie notices that she's not wearing her pearls, that she's deliberately refrained from flouting her wealth: it is with other weapons she wishes to fight for her man. But pearls can pass on from one woman to a man without the man being 'effeminate'. The famous opening scene of *Chéri* has Chéri decked with Léa's pearls, fighting for her to give them to him – as a sign of love, as the crowning of his beauty, a tribute to his love-making, a kind of inheritance from his 'Nounoune'. Conversely, Léa keeps her pearls, wears them, even in bed, as a shield for age: they hide her ageing neck. When Colette met Maurice Goudeket, he was a dealer in pearls, an expert in pearls: that was at least five years after she'd written *Chéri*...

Chéri's baths and clothes are as elaborate as Léa's. His care for 'toilette' is part of what makes him such a wonderful lover. Julie de Carneilhan polishes her boots and grooms horses as well as any man. Degrees of what is called femininity *and* of what is called masculinity exist in almost all of Colette's female characters, as well as in most of her male characters. It is a matter of infinitely complex negotiations, and none of it has a value *in itself*. For instance, in *Le Toutounier*, the 'masculine' sister Colombe and the 'feminine' one Hermine *both* smoke, both earn a living, both wear make-up and borrow it from each other. And they both love their men with absolute passion, the 'masculine' one being prepared to give up everything to follow her man, the 'feminine' one attempting to shoot her rival in a bid for her lover. And yet, both – in fact, all three sisters, for new distinctions would be required to speak also of Alice, the third sister – all three sisters come out as excitingly, vividly 'womanly'. And the relationship that binds all three as a kind of relationship that could only bind women.

Language and currency

Colette's pursuit in her writing of the materiality and individuality of words seems to me to be continuous with her attitude to objects, gender, values. She once wrote to a young friend who wanted some advice on the matter that a word only becomes new thanks to its nearness to another word that renews it. That seems to me characteristic. The search for identity and specificity is through relationships. The mystery of meaning, of feeling, of self, is pursued actively through the use of syntax, word groupings, images, in which the word is always unique but also involved in changing operations with others. I remember my delight, when reading the piece about the storm which Toby-Chien watches cowering under his mistress's sofa, and coming upon his almost horizontal vision of the large and violent drops of rain spattering the sand, which is 'gaufré' by them. Wafered, that is, punched with regular holes like the French biscuits called 'gaufres' or 'gaufrettes'. It gave me such a beautifully precise vision, as if I had been the dog, peering terrified from between the tassels. And so I was startled when I found the same verb used in *Creature Conversations* turned to quite a different but equally precise effect in *Chéri*. Léa has been sleeping in her armchair, her cheek pressed against a cushion, and she wakes up. As she rises from her chair, she rubs 'her cheek, embossed by the imprint of the embroidered cushion'(110). 'Embossed by the imprint', in the French, is 'gaufré'. The verb conveys the limited space of the pitting that has taken place (the embossed cheek is about as large as a 'gaufrette'), and it is poised between touch and sight. Léa's finger identifies a wafer texture on her cheek, and the reader half feels it, half sees it in his or her turn.

This is just a tiny example of what goes on all the time in Colette's prose. Take a paragraph at random: it would be hard to find two sentences that have the same construction, the same pace. This seems to me to stem from the way in which value, for Colette, is never predetermined. In which objects and places and people require ceaseless readjustments to be seen or felt. Well, that is so in Proust or Virginia Woolf. But there is more materiality, less 'consciousness' as innerness in Colette, and things are more stable in her universe than in either of the other two novelists. A bizarrely subversive conservative, she remains out there, in the world such as it is, the world of Capital and of the exchange of women – of currencies. She writes in a way that is *current*. True, some readers have difficulty with the form of some of her later books: *The Break of Day, The Evening Star, The Blue Lantern,* even *The Pure and the Impure*, which she thought was a book 'without a subject', a book she would have liked to have called *Remous – Currents, Eddies*. Pity she did not choose that title for a book so close in its date of writing to Woolf's *The Waves*. The two women did not know each other: would they have seen the point of each other's book, and form? But even readers who do not like those later books of Colette would agree that they are easy to read, they would not think of them as 'experimental' or 'modernist'. (Which in my opinion they are.) They would say, 'The book meanders too much', or, 'This is not worthy of Colette'.

The kind of currency at work in Colette's prose might be made perceptible by contrast with a writer who strikes me as the opposite of Colette: Simone de Beauvoir.

Her opposite: because she rejected the traditional world of womanhood, that 'domestic circle' that Colette chose to animate, and went for these male preserves – Literature, Philosophy, Freedom, Politics – which Colette never manifested the slightest interest in. The projection towards a world of meaning, for Simone de Beauvoir, is tantamount to living in an eternal future. Its effect, to my mind, is to desiccate the world of things, what is traditionally the province of the feminine. She may vibrate when she is 'discovering' books, getting to 'know' landscapes, avidly, through travelling. But travel and movement, of the eye, the pen, the body, there must be: so that when she evokes a childhood place which she claims actually to have loved, the stasis of the place, in her prose, produces a *list*:

The most lively place in the house was the kitchen, which took up half the basement... I loved the massive wood of the table, the benches, the sideboards. The ironcast stove threw flames. The copper pans glittered: saucepans of all sizes, cauldrons, skimmers, basins, warming-pans; I rejoiced in the gaiety of the enamel dishes with their childish colours, the variety of bowls, cups, glasses, porringers, butter-dishes, pots, jugs, pitchers. Cast-iron, earthenware, sandstone, china, aluminium, tin, how many cooking-pots, frying-pans, casserole-pots, stewpots, cassoulet-pans, soup-pots, dishes, tumblers, sieves, choppers, mills, moulds, mortars![4]

Translating this myself from the French rather than looking up the translation, I have of course become aware that the area of cooking and eating utensils is perhaps one of the few in which the French language is richer than the English: hence the difficulty of rendering some words. But that is a minor part of the trouble with this passage. It is well-timed, well-managed, in something like the naturalist tradition, down to the final alliteration: 'mills, moulds, mortars'. But in the midst of celebrating the liveliness of the kitchen, the author seems to be overwhelmed by a feeling she has many times elsewhere, the feeling of meaningless accumulation, as when she imagines her mother's days in the kitchen (and the fate that awaits her if she becomes like her mother) as an infinite series of grey boxes. Or when she is sickened by a sense of the infinite repetition of identical blades of grass. The strength of her revulsion from anything to do with mothering or nurture cuts the bond between herself and objects – you might almost say, between herself and people. Her relationships, as she writes about them, always seem to me to be occurring with half of herself entranced, or half of herself turned off. The list of the kitchen implements, however celebratory in intention and accurate in its naming, has the effect of reducing them all to the same status, without relation to each other and to the narrator, who's certainly never been interested in the various meanings of 'timbale' (which can be a christening cup, a simple metal cup, a tumbler, a mould or a timbale dish), in the fact that it's a more unusual thing to have several mortars or mills than frying-pans, or in the way in which the elements of that list might be used to produce a meal.

A simple sentence by Colette, producing a glimpse of a kitchen, gives me more of a sense of what kind of a kitchen we are dealing with, what's going on in it, who works there, what food comes out of it, than Simone de Beauvoir's much more detailed list. That is because each word exists independently, for its own sake, involving an active, precise knowledge of what it is. And because words interact instead of being serialized:

> Only Mme Suzanne's bust could be seen, each time the kitchen hatch opened, framing her golden hair and her flushed face on a background of furbished basins and fish-grills shaped like hoop-nets. (B-V: 140, my translation)[5]

You're in Provence, near the sea: that type of fish-grill is characteristic. Mme Suzanne is a Northerner, she comes from Paris, she's got golden hair, she's comfortable, warm like her own baking ('toute chaude', which I've translated as 'flushed', is also hot, as if she were bread still hot from the oven, and therefore delectable), her cooking is appetizing, she likes it, she generates a pleasing sense of nurture in her guests at the boarding-house. There is also something Flemish in Mme Suzanne's roseate bulk and in the way in which the hatch *frames* her, and the basins are furbished. Indeed, later on in the story, a contingent of Belgian guests will stop at the *pension*, and will love it.

It is as if Colette, by accepting the currency of language, the currency of money, the currency of bodies, by staying, as it were, inside the system, found ways of emancipating whatever she touches – objects, people, relationships – from alienation. 'With Usura hath no man a house of good stone,' Pound was thundering at the time when Colette was writing *Bella-Vista*. In the cleanliness with which Julie de Carneilhan handles the pink and blue notes, as in the well-cut edges of her sentences and paragraphs and books, Colette the craftswoman with a Jewish husband she did her best to protect in the war years was doing more to restore clean values to life than the noisy brigades of the self-appointed purifiers of language.

Chapter Ten

De-Fetishizing Writing

The materiality of language

Ever since what's been called 'the death of God',
somewhere between Romanticism and Symbolism, in
the course of the nineteenth century, the figure of the
artist has taken on religious proportions it never quite
had before. He comes to rank among the 'grands initiés',
the magi and prophets who led mankind into the Great
Beyond, the Unknown. He is an heir not just to
Orpheus, but to Christ. Dante might gain access to
Paradise, travel through the rose in centripetal circles,
ever-closer to the heart of light. Still, the system of faith
that upheld and informed his *Divine Comedy* made him
very humble as well as a privileged seer. That system
was gone, and with it the hierarchy that gave its place to
the individual, and their depths to moral and artistic
values, when Symbolist poets in France, treading in the
steps of their Romantic models, erected the figure of the
poet into that of 'a voyant', a man charged with priestly

functions, but working in a vacuum of values, throwing
the dice of writing on the eternal desert of the white
page. What he wrote tended towards what Mallarmé
called 'The Book', the 'Orphic interpretation of the earth',
which, religion having collapsed, only the artist could
now undertake. He was now responsible for Meaning.
Words had to be found, that could lead Mankind. The
'horrible labourers' who found them, like Rimbaud, had
to spend a season in Hell. There was no breaking through
to Purgatory, no ascent of Mount Purgatory towards
the earthly Paradise. That was behind, lost, with childhood. Full-stop. Except for the terrifying short glimpses
the martyred Poet afforded us. The stakes of Literature
had become absolute. Salvation was now part and parcel
of the art of writing.

We're still paddling in all this, like babies in a Butlin's
pool rather than like ducks in a lake. Let alone swans, Oh
Lord, deliver us from symbolic swans. For salvation
through writing came cunningly to assume all forms. It
could be individual, as in Proust: writing one's life would
redeem it, the artist-as-scientist would research time, the
artist-as-explorer would find time, the artist-as-writer
would ring time, link by link, and the magic of words
would hold it fast. It could be political, anarchic, as with
Dada, or revolutionary, as with the Surrealists. It could
be philosophical, face up to and express the absurdity of
Man's fate, thus becoming the one act that posits
freedom, again and again, each act of writing, each act of
reading defeating the Absurd while it lasts, pushing
Sisyphus's rock up the mountain although you know it
will tumble down again.

Colette was born when Rimbaud was writing his
Illuminations (1873). She worked on *Claudine At School*
before Verlaine died, while Mallarmé was still active,
and *L'Ingénue libertine* is contemporary with Gide's *la Porte*

Etroite and *L'Immoraliste*. *Chéri* co-dates the productions of Duchamp and Tzara, *The Last of Chéri* and *The Ripening Seed* the Surrealist Manifestos. *Bella-Vista* and *La Chatte* are roughly of the same years as Sartre's *La Nausée* and Camus's *The Outsider*. And the lady was working on *The Evening Star* and *The Blue Lantern* when Sartre was penning *Being and Nothingness* and *What is Literature?*, and his girlfriend Simone reading at the Bibliothèque Sainte-Geneviève to document a book that was eventually to be called *The Second Sex*. That same Simone had been born in the years in which a rather obscure mime called Colette Willy was writing *The Vagabond* in her *loge*, in between rehearsal and performance and while a miner's son called D.H. Lawrence was working on *Women In Love*. But unlike Colette Willy, Simone de Beauvoir was never fond of her own body. She entered Literature as one might enter religion, giving herself up, body and soul, to the sacralization of writing. Colette seems to have sailed through the whole period with a gleeful pagan disregard of all those 'salvations' – religious, atheistic or political. Yet I would contend that her prose is inferior to none of those 'great contemporaries'.

In her decided indifference to the sacralization of writing, Colette departs again from 'male' models to create something that is very much her own.

Fetishism is the act whereby you invest an object with magical properties. In *The Mill on The Floss*, Maggie Tulliver makes her doll into a fetish, driving nails into it and banging its wooden head on the walls to vent her grief at the way she's been treated, or her aggression against the grown-ups. Marx uses a table as an example of the fetishism of commodities, born of the expansion of Capital, whereby a thing ceases to be a thing regarded for its use-value. The table loses its materiality, its wooden-ness and shape and the craft that's made it, it is no longer seen as an object to eat or write on, and it starts 'evolving out of its wooden brain grotesque ideas' that derive from its exchange-value. In Freud, a child who is struggling in the grip of the castration complex, transfers his protectiveness from his penis to his feet, and becomes highly susceptible about his toes: his ego has split. He thinks he has preserved both his 'penis' and his ability to masturbate, which is what he had been forbidden to do in the first place, with the implied fatherly threat, 'If you don't stop, I'll cut it off'. And in the process his toes have become fetishized. You could argue that when Mallarmé imbues the white page, the black ink, with a total symbolical significance, he is in effect fetishizing the act of writing. Black and white, dark and light, writing implements, evolve out of their paper or liquid brains grotesque ideas, and start dancing on their heads like Marx's table. They dance so well, that the white page becomes elevated to the heights of the starry skies. So said Valéry about Mallarmé's 'Coup de dés'.

It may be unfair to link the fetishization of writing so closely with Capital, and the discovery of the subconscious. Ronsard, the French Renaissance poet, for instance, wrote a lovely sonnet on his death-bed, in which he bid good-bye to pots and pans, houses and gardens, sang his swan-song, but with the knowledge that his quill would fly up to Heaven to become a 'Signe', or 'Cygne', a sign/swan/Cygnus. Talk about the exchange-value of sounds in language! The man Ronsard's life may have been ebbing fast, but he had lost none of his verbal skill. Still, there would be nothing there to stop Gilbert and Gubar from adding old Ronsard to their collection of male authors who, with Lord Rochester as their raucous interpreter, felt they wrote with their 'piffle' (and that ladies should not pretend they have one). But I would contend that there was an element of play in Ronsard, or a trusting reference to a whole mythological and therefore in some ways *social* universe, which made such fetishization less absolute, less desperate, than many Modernist ways of worshipping 'l'écriture'. There is, however, no denying that art has always had complicated relations to 'totem'.

Colette was born before Marx died. She was younger than Freud, but she became famous at an early age, and we have seen that *Claudine At School* came out the same year as *Dora*. It was written in the period in which Freud was studying hysterics and working on *The Interpretation of Dreams*. She was interested in neither, and probably never opened one of their books.

Is it on account of that total disregard of theory (or because she was that kind of person anyway) that, although she was aware of the contemporary literary scene (Naturalism, Symbolism, Decadence, etc.), being right in the middle of it thanks to Willy, she never went for bookish talk. Later, when as Mme de Jouvenel she was a *salon* hostess, she insisted on talking about plants or animals or cooking.[1] Even later, when Sartre and Simone de Beauvoir sat at Colette's feet, you can imagine the expression on their faces when the grand old lady of French letters talked to them about truffles or the fertilizing properties of seaweeds, and explained to them how to bake crusts of bread-and-butter over 'café-au-lait'. I can certainly picture the glint in her cat-like eyes if anyone had spoken of 'l'écriture' reverently in front of her.

Colette was always fond of food. And became more so in her old age. Raymond Oliver, the famous 'chef' of the Grand Véfour, has written a lovely account of his good relations with his 'gourmande' neighbour of the Palais-Royal. It is striking, in the face of quills flying up to

Heaven and white paper becoming frozen lakes, that in
Claudine At School what the heroine and her friends do
with pens and paper is to... eat them. They also make
hair-curlers with school exercise-books. 'La grande
Anaïs' has a perverse and omnivorous appetite for all
writing implements:

> ... Anaïs takes advantage of the commotion to pinch me,
> and pull devilish faces while munching charcoal and india-
> rubber ... all day long her pockets and mouth are filled with
> the wood of pencils, with black, filthy rubber, with charcoal
> and pink blotting paper. Chalk, black lead, she stuffs herself
> with it; it's all that food, no doubt, that gives her a
> complexion the colour of grey wood and plaster. I only eat
> cigarette paper, and only a special brand. (*C At S*: 22, my
> translation)

If Colette never wanted to write when she was a young
girl, she was still fascinated by writing implements. She
has portrayed that fascination in *Green Wax*, where the
child Colette covets the wonderful tools on her father's
desk, the pens and pencils and exquisite ink-pots and
rubbers and waxes, with the passion of a budding
craftswoman. That love of writing as craft, the pleasure
to be derived from the materials with which you do it,
and the skill which you apply to it, will be with her
always. Indeed, her description of the feel and look of the
exercise-books she bought to write *Claudine At School*
suggests that her pleasure in dealing with that kind of
ruled and feinted paper had much to do with her ability
to ink it with her round and legible hand. Her
schoolmistress, the real one, had insisted on the
neatness and legibility of the hand her pupils wrote, and
Colette kept to that lesson. Also, the strong, heavily-
bound cover protected her: she was not yet venturing
into the bird-space of the fly-leaf. But she also indulged

in the extreme pleasure that fine paper and fine writing one). But I would contend that there was an element of implements gave her. She loved beautiful letter-writing paper, she got used to writing her books on blue paper. In *Bella-Vista*, her *alter ego* of an author has brought a kilo of periwinkle paper in her suitcase. That is also the paper she drapes over her writing-lamp in the late years, to make it into her 'blue boat-light'. This is barely a metaphor. With her paralysed hips she is truly ship-wrecked on her 'raft', drifting at nights in her reverie over sleeping Paris, yet there always, safe and watching, a tiny but protective sign in the great sea of the city. What a difference between that light, and the 'lueur étroite de [la] lampe', Mallarmé's narrow beam of light on the empty paper 'que sa blancheur défend': defended or made into a forbidden thing, by its whiteness.

Black and white

There is a steady refusal in Colette of that black and white dichotomy, too. I have talked about the way she made one/two, the One/the Other types of opposition inoperative: between superior and inferior, animal and human, male and female. She won't entertain either those images that bore the 'myth' of writing at the turn of the century. In Valéry, for instance, a male god, a form-giver, a holy fit, a spirit of negation, Apollo or Serpent, invests a female body which is akin to 'Nature', a Pythoness, or Eve. The space that is thus occupied is a virgin female space: white.

Speech, writing, are male acts that help the Subject come into being. Colette is not interested in that kind of inscription. Her writing is continuous with, and expressive of, her own body at all sorts of levels, but not symbolically. There is a very nice correction of hers to the proof of the inside title page of *The Ripening Seed*: she wants clearer and fatter types for the name 'Colette'. She also wants no capitals for the title, she wants it to be 'le blé en herbe'. When corn is still in shoots, it's not reached the capital stage, any more than her adolescents, Phil and Vinca, have. And she knew that the name 'Colette' was now a substantial one: Colette the woman herself had grown quite bulky.

She is not interested in virginity, in spaces or on paper any more than in women. The creative moments in her work are those in which the woman at last knows pleasure, finds love, its wildness and uncertainties, or takes, as Léa and Julie de Carneilhan do, a brave and creative decision. And her texts are two-sexed. Or rather, as we have seen, she occupies all the positions of love, actually and imaginatively, from the female to the male adolescent, from the virile to the 'feminine' woman, from the very young to the very old lover (from Chéri and Phil to Renaud, or the seducer of *The Tender Shoot*), from the female to the male homosexual. You have to talk about a spectrum, not about an opposition. And pleasure, for her, is multiple, not One, nor orgasmic in a thunder-and-lightning, tongues of flame way. Ripples, and sometimes breakers, but always the sea, the sea. Pleasure is multiple: 'Remous' . . . for the first title of what became later *The Pure and The Impure, Ces Plaisirs*. . . . Colette was citing her own *The Ripening Seed*: 'those pleasures, which are wrongly called physical'. She plotted a comic chapter that would have been called 'Unisexuelles'; the subtitle would have been: 'Chapitre unique'. And its entire content: 'Il n'y a pas d'unisexuelles'.[2]

Colette writes black on blue, or on mauve, or dark blue on light blue. No 'hydra' vomits on the purity of the white page. Writing is something quite specific, which her mother did sitting on a bale of hay in the barn at home or with a cat pawing at the pen. She did it noisily, scratching at the paper as she might have scratched at the earth, or at the skin of a potato. Indeed, *The Break of Day* where this description of Sido writing occurs, is one of the books most obviously concerned with writing: Colette's own hand, short, stubby, strong, with callouses and its nails broken by energetic gardening, is the hand that both pushes a pen and finds its own reflection by touching a young man's tanned chest. A very active narcissism, if that is the right word, in which the writerly self perceives itself not by catching the 'echo of [its] internal greatness' (as in Valéry's 'Le Cimetière marin'), nor through contemplation of its own image in the surface of some mirror, but as a good worker's hand comfortably touching skin, earth, paper. The activity is hard. It takes a lot of self-imposed discipline. At La Treille Muscate where she is writing *The Break of Day*, Colette sits at a desk facing the angle of two walls, as if she were still a child in the 'quadrangular nook' in the bookcase at home'³ or being set an imposition by Melle Sergent, or by Willy. The various ages of life through which you become a good craftswoman gather there, in another spectrum of time: schoolgirl and mature woman, Sido's little daughter and independent worker marked by age.

Willy had taught her that every letter counts, that you must hound 'coquilles', misprints. The whole punning milieu of her apprenticeships had shown what difference an 'r' to 'merde' can make. Any mutation in the writing body, also, was communicated to the writing hand. With the onset of fever, the 'jambages', the legs of 'j' and 'p' and 'g' shiver, multiply, the text begins to see double. Colette, in all sorts of ways, resurrects lost yet evident links between the body and language.

And she manages to write 'realistically' enjoyable texts in a prose that is as cunning as that of more difficult ones. Barthes's distinction between consumable texts and experimental ones that defend themselves against being understood is invalid: you cannot call Colette 'readerly' *nor* 'writerly'. She is both, it's all a question of how you read. At a simple but essential level, she makes a call, not upon the reader's cleverness, but on her/his willingness to discover what s/he knows.

The kingdom of beasts, and more generally what is called 'nature', we destroy, tame, ignore. It is the kingdom whose specificity Colette seems keenest to convey, freest to convey too, in her early work. Kiki-la-Doucette and Toby-Chien were perhaps free from Willy's interference, being beneath his notice if not his liking: and Toby-Chien being, like his mistress, exploited for his publicity potential, he was a companion in misfortune, someone who could be invested with the potential that Colette reined in under her master's stick. And so we have *Dialogue de bêtes*. During the Great War, we have *La Paix chez les bêtes*, animals surviving in the nooks and crannies of what was called civilization, or the fight for it, tits building in the mouths of idle canons and toms pursuing their wild nightly conquests in the back-gardens round smart Neuilly. There even is a sense that in that period at least, animals become invested for Colette with what is normally put into religion. In *La Paix chez les bêtes*, there is a Christmas tale for the children of the 'poilus'. A human, therefore fur-less despite his iron-ical name of 'poilu', 'hairy', the soldier is almost dying of the cold and of depression in his night-trench, under all the cloaks and blankets he's been able to find. He is magically visited by all the furry creatures, a colt, an otter, a rabbit, a marten, offering their fur to protect him. He keens for the magnificent white coat of a she-cat:

... the White Cat alighted on his blanket, like a snowflake
fluttering down. Her crystalline purring vibrated all through
her, and her fur was shot with the vague, pale, rainbow
colours that are imprisoned in sprays of spun glass. ...

"Pass your hand along my back," went on the Cat.
"A crackling fire will follow your palm, as phosphorescent
water outlines the footsteps of one who walks at night
upon a moist seashore. Would you like me to spread out my
tail peacock-wise, but in a fan of sparks instead of
feathers?" (*CGS:* 316–317)

In the morning, when the 'poilu' wakes up, a meta-
morphosis has occurred: he is covered by a shimmering,
warm, thick white fur. It is snow. He shakes it off as he
springs to battle, but heat and courage have coated his
heart, as if the powers of the fur had gone magically
inwards.

That story Colette re-wrote, with a different protagonist, a child, a naughty child, who in the thick of the
night sees all the objects and creatures he has hurt or
maltreated during the day come to life: they hound him
in their turn, and he learns to respect the mystery of life.
Ravel set this to music: it is called, *L'Enfant et les sortilèges*.
Nature is no 'Grandame Earth' for Colette, nor a 'deep
chasm' in which 'the Imagination of the whole' speaks
'with the voice of roaring torrents', nor steep mountains
nor Wild West Wind nor Temple with living pillars. It's
more to do with a Persian cat whose green eyes have the
hue of the greyish underside of willow leaves, or the
passion with which Mr Donzague's little sow ploughs up
truffles with her little snout out of red Limousin earth,
in a spitting drizzle that turns to rain: and the smell that
rises from the bucketful of truffles afterwards, when
Mr. Donzague and his visitors warm up near a wood fire
at an inn. Each creature has its specific, its unique life

and beauty. Each demands that it be looked at for what it is, without categories or prejudices. Each, above all, invites to a different sort of relationship, inevitably fraught with social and cultural evils, like the captured grass-snakes, the 'couleuvres' which Colette buys from a cageful of entangled snakes. She cannot release them into the garden for the cats would tear them to pieces. And so she handles them, she wrestles with them, feels their girth, their coldness, their smoothness, their dryness, their surprise at her warmth, their anger, fear, their dawning acceptance. A relationship. A complex, distinct relationship, is what is sought with each creature. As Colette went on to write, became more confident, the relationships with *humans*, which in *The Vagabond* and *The Shackle* had begun to develop with increased economy and delicacy, become charged with the specificity, tact and watchfulness that were in the relationships with woods or animals in the earlier year. From *Chéri* onwards, through *The Ripening Seed, Duo, The Other One, The Toutonier, Julie de Carneilhan*, the flair that informed Colette's watchfulness of animals, passes into her dealings with humans. Many of the exchanges have to be glimpsed or divined. The mystery of self remains potent. The reader has to develop a kind of sixth sense, animal senses, a sharper nose or a keener sight.

The signs and implements of writing, black and white, then, take on a different dimension in Colette from those they have in most of her (largely male) contemporaries. Her writing labours at reconstituting the woof and web, what connects language to the world, instead of seeking black-and-white oppositions, of seeing language as what signals the 'death' or disappearance of the world: unlike Mallarmé or Blanchot. Unlike Sartre.

And so, the world becomes peopled by things which write. There are multiple forms of writing, from the sinuous signs the grass-snakes' bodies make as they grapple with, become accustomed to, the body of their mistress, to the musical notes that the steps of the iron staircase leading to the underground dressing-rooms make in *Gribiche*: 'the last five steps each gave out their particular note like a xylophone – B, B flat, C, D and then dropping a fifth to G' (*SC*: 67). Mediocre humans make signs that are quickly erased: the stain left by the Haumes in *Chance Acquaintances* is of the kind that grows faint with time. Writing is, among other things, deciphering the writing of life, and seeking for signs delicate enough to come close to secret tragedy without doing it violence:

> When I felt that I wanted to write the story of Gribiche, I controlled myself and replaced it by a 'blank', a row of dots, an asterisk. Today ... I ... surround [her] memory with the emblems of silence. Among such emblems are those which, in musical notation, signify the breaking-off of the melody. Three hieroglyphs can indicate that break: a mute swallow on the five black wires of the stave; a tiny hatchet cutting across them, and – for the longest pause of all – a fixed pupil under a huge, arched, panic-stricken eyebrow. (*SC*: 104)

Music has taken over from silence. Through musical signs, Colette moves towards the writing beyond writing that Sido's last scrawls had made her glimpse.

'Blank' can lead into non-linguistic signs, or suggestions, as music in Verlaine merged into silence. But also, white is not white. It is not just blue, or mauve, either. The fur of the white cat in the Christmas tale for the 'poilus' is electric, shimmering, a world of iridescent colours. It is not just like snow, which instead of whiteness and ice releases warmth in the tale, becomes a fur, binds the soldier to nurturing forces. Instead of being a stage on which the authorial self that seeks for identity through inscription, murders reality in the process: it is like the paper on which the writer writes which can reveal a shimmering reality.

Chapter Eleven

Autobiography as Prism:
Rainy Moon

All of Colette's works occupy a complicated, and in each case different place in the spectrum that goes from the red of autobiography to the purple of fiction. She was never interested in invention for its own sake, and never moves away from what she knows at first-hand. Her fiction never lets go the hand of her own life. But she hated confessional modes and thought the embattled notion of truthfulness too immodest ever to write 'pure' autobiography. A version of self is at stake in every single text she wrote, but it straddles the relation between 'art' and 'life' in a way that is quite special. This is particularly true of her late, long stories. I'll call them 'novellas', which is a term used for Lawrence's *The Captain's Doll* for instance: stories long enough to allow for the play of casualness. There is more casualness of course in Colette than in Lawrence. Indeed, she calls her novellas 'blancs': they are white, the blanks in a woman's life, her life. They're the whites between chapters in a book. A revealing notion, in an author who always had short chapters: regular breathing, systole and diastole. The blacks, she says, correspond to the period in which she was in love, when love so preoccupied her that the rest of the world disappeared. The novels came out of the love: *The Shackle, Chéri, The Other One.*

Whites, on the contrary, are periods in which nothing happens, in between two loves. When the narrator, often at a loss, takes notice of what is happening to others, people she is not even involved with, who are casual acquaintances: as in *Le Képi, Chambre d'hôtel* (pointedly translated *Chance Acquaintances*), *Bella-Vista, Gribiche,* whose musical white I have evoked in the previous chapter, *The Tender Shoot,* and others. The narrator is often in between homes: in a hotel (*Chance Acquaintances*) or a *pension* (*Bella-Vista*). Randomness in the telling, digressions, interruptions, are part and parcel of the tale. Indeed, you could say that 'white' is also the reverse of the 'black' of detective fiction, in which you read for clues, and look for passages that are particularly significant. In Colette's novellas, everything appears to be vaguely unimportant, meandering, and at the same time *everything* can be read as significant. You are distorting if you isolate bits to construct arguments around them, since the air of unimportance, chance, is what comes across. So it is not easy to write about these white stories. In them, nothing happens to the narrator/protagonist. She is going through a genuinely hollow moment in her life. The depth is in the surface, the opening out of a spectrum: in *Rainy Moon*, in paying close attention, because you are bored, to the exact pattern and reflection of light upon a wallpaper.

Rainy Moon is exemplary. Like the other novellas, it posits the identity of author, narrator and protagonist, fulfilling all the conditions which Philippe Lejeune has helpfully laid out as characteristic of autobiography.[1] It is a retrospective prose narration, dealing with an individual life, and the reader is prepared to make a 'contract' with the *author's name*. That name is famous, the reader believes in the identity that is being proposed.

Mme Colette, the protagonist then, is a fairly established writer who brings her stories to a professional typist. The typist is a spinster called Rosita Barberet. It turns out that she lives in a flat in Montmartre in which the narrator herself lived, an unspecified number of years before. The narrator is moved by the recognition, all the more so as it appears that her former bedroom, in which she spent solitary waiting hours after the breakdown of a marriage, is now occupied by the typist's young sister, Délia, who also spends solitary hours there, waiting for her husband. As she brings writing to the typist, the narrator gets more and more drawn to Délia, as to another self or the double of her former self. She mothers her, wants to give her advice, tries to confess her, finds her more undecipherable than a child. Her interpretative instincts are called out, but to no avail. She also protects the mystery that is puzzling her, since she won't tell her best friend, Annie de Pène, a perspicacious woman, about her visits to the Barberet sisters. One day, the narrator, who has gone down into the street to buy cherries for Délia, meets a young man looking up towards Délia's window, and from Délia's reaction when she's told about the young man, understands that he was Délia's husband, Eugène. Another time, she walks into the Barberets' dark entrance and almost stumbles over Délia, who is lying across the floor. Then Délia takes to fine needlepoint. Meanwhile, her sister Rosita is more and more disturbed, drops dark hints. She finally visits the narrator in *her* flat, and reveals to her that Délia is weaving a spell to kill her husband. The narrator has stumbled across a case of witchcraft in twentieth-century Paris. A frequent event, Rosita intimates. The narrator discards the revelation, but she gets rid of her own stories, loses touch with the two sisters. One day, while she is coming back from the flea-market with Annie de Pène, she catches sight of Délia, gleefully eating chips in the street: she is in black, deep mourning that is almost purple; cupping her little chin is 'the white crêpe band of a widow'.

Time inhabits the story in layers, to do not only with the series of selves the narrator encounters inside the story, but also with the moment in which she is telling it. 'Colours of a prism' might be a better term than 'layers', since 'rainy moon', which gives the story its title, is an effect produced by the diffraction of light, a rainbow globe of light projected on the wallpaper in the flat. As the narrator first penetrates into the flat, she has a moment of involuntary memory when her hand touches the window latch on which it so often rested when she was a young wife waiting for a lost husband. It is shaped like a siren, and becomes the occasion for deep-sea diving: not once, as in Proust (who is specifically evoked), but several times. The recognition of the 'rainy moon' is another such Proustian moment. When it is first seen, it seems a beneficent phenomenon, combining, with poetic quizzicality, two elements, rain and moon, that have an obscure correlation: the moon, the reader may speculate, draws the waters, causes the tides. Moon and storms are often associated: yet through its rainbow effect, the tiny globe suggests harmony, reconciliation. The reader, speculating some more, can associate it with the author's taste for prismatic glass paper-weights: indeed, when the narrator visits the flea-market with Annie, this may be one of the objects she has been looking for. The biographer would rightly tell us that Annie had begun Colette's collection of paper-weights. Colette, writing the story in 1940, over twenty years after Annie's death, may have looked at them and remembered...

What I am doing is opening out the possibilities of meaning as one opens a fan, making appear the hidden folds of the 'real' author behind those that the narrator/protagonist show. The posited identity of all three enables me to do that, yet more meanings come to light as you separate them, place them side by side, rather. The Proustian moments can also make the reader associate the rainy moon with the magic lantern that illuminates the narrator's childhood bedroom in Combray, seeming to hold iridescent promise of the future.

At any rate, to the narrator first perceiving it, rainy moon is friendly. As the story unfolds, and Délia's black magic overtakes the narrator's own illusion of, or reliance upon, white magic (the signs and portents that interest her, in the weather as on a human face, and by means of which she tries to read reality), the prism becomes maleficent, a thing of the night, as is the moon, after all. 'A blind alley haunted by evil designs, was this what had become of the little flat where once I had suffered without bitterness, watched over by my rainy moon?' (SC: 198–9). Purple, which turns out as the colour of Délia's mourning, is the seventh colour of the prism, and Rosita warns the narrator that, six moons have already passed since Délia began her maleficent vigil, the seventh, which is coming, will be the death of Eugène, whom she, Rosita the pink or red, has in vain tried to save from her sister.[2] Purple, incidentally, is the colour of the folder in which the love-letter that drives Michel to insane jealousy in *Duo*, is hidden: it is a peculiar combination of light, illuminating both the folder and a bunch of violet orchids and casting its glow on Alice, that draws Michel's attention to the folder Alice is trying to conceal from him.

The spectrum of the rainbow functions in many ways. One of these is time. *Rainy Moon*, to start with, takes place at an unspecified period. It seems that many years must separate the time in which the narrator inhabited the flat, and that in which she revisits it. The recognition of the lay-out of the rooms, and of the staircase leading up to the flat, seems to come very far. One of Colette's rare recounted dreams concerns the staircase of one of the many houses she lived in and it comes to haunt her when she is writing *The Evening Star* (1946), not so very long after *Rainy Moon* (1940). There is a sense of psychic depth, resonances from a long way off, in the phenomena of involuntary memory that occur. When I first read the story, I thought it was meant to take place at the same time as *Bella-Vista*, round about 1924, which was one of her 'blank' periods. The narrator/protagonist feels mature, though she is less well-established as a writer than in *Bella-Vista*. Rosita, who is middle-aged and very proper, is highly respectful. The protagonist herself is motherly and confident both to Rosita and to Délia. Yet the story must clearly be 'dated' as taking place around 1910 at the latest. Not only did Annie de Pène, with whom 'Colette' goes on cheerful cycling expeditions, die in 1918, but Sido, who comes to spend a few days in Paris with her daughter in the middle of the story, providing a refreshing distraction from what has already become an unhealthy fascination, died in 1912. And the author/narrator had not yet met the man who was to rescue her from lovelessness and become her second husband, in 1911. At the same time, the period of waiting and pining for a lost husband, that is being resurrected for the narrator by her visit to the Barberet flat, cannot be any earlier than 1906, since only then did Colette leave Willy. So the 'actual' chronology at which one arrives is four years at the most. But there are signs of a much more considerable lapse of years than that: the entire row of houses across the street has been pulled down, so that the view from the windows is quite changed. The house in which the Barberets live has been entirely replastered from the outside, and the vestibule redecorated, the shops have changed owners, the former 'crèmerie' now sells accordions and banjos. The corner sweet-shop has been repainted; but the lady who sells them is no longer blonde and blue, she is grey-haired and wears mauve (another few hues of the spectrum there). However she still sells black liquorice sweets called 'petits pains de Tortosa' (nicely translated as 'Pontefract cakes'), whose taste is so strong that it spoils the flavour of everything else. As does, on and off, the narrator's fascination for the Barberets. They act in the story as another instance of the 'madeleine'.

What I am trying to show is that it is impossible to read that story within the strict terms of identity of author/narrator/protagonist that the autobiographical pact posits. If one does, the chronology becomes severely strained (how can the sweet-lady have aged so drastically in four years?), and the interplay between the present of the author/narrator and the various layers of the past that are being brought out of the depths by the narrator/protagonist are squashed flat. At the same time, the presence of the autobiographical pact, and the way in which Colette's texts unfurl when biography is fed into them, make it difficult for the reader not to root the story into the author's actual, known past. All the more so as Colette herself plays with this: she also writes about Annie de Pène in other texts that she labels 'memoirs', she feeds in her own persona as a now famous writer. For instance, you feel that the author knows that the reader is going to wonder about those stories of hers that she erased or threw away at the end of the Barberet connection. The novella functions like the rainy moon itself, the basic chronology (1906–10) being *diffracted* by means of it into a lived chronology that goes from 1906 to 1940. It may well be that the idea of the story itself was suggested by a recent, accidental visit to the former flat, or the area where it was.

As well as that, there are concealed, 'blank' elements of the 1906–10 chronology at work. There are *two* sisters living together, the one, Rosita, reliable and plain, brutally aged by her sister's wickedness, the other pretty, evil and passionate. Is there in that relationship a shadow of that which existed then between Missy and Colette? Colette, after all, ruthlessly dumped Missy when she fell in love with Jouvenel: despite the autobiographical contract, Missy is totally erased from the tale, and the protagonist lives alone. Also, the story of a woman – Délia – who kills her husband by willing him dead whilst she is inhabiting the bedroom of a woman, the narrator who, when she, as author, writes, had waited for *two* husbands who had left her, has a strange significance. All the more so as Délia 'convoque', summons, her husband by calling his name, Eugène: and as the narrator remembers herself at that window also calling a man's first name. If you, the reader, aware of Colette's biography, remember Willy's first name, you'll know at once it was 'Henry' – which was also Henry de Jouvenel's first name... and the author had already written a scene like it: Renée, at the end of *The Shackle*, desperately summons the man she loves and fear she's lost, calling his name, 'Jean' – at a window...

Rainy Moon is the only one of Colette's novels or novellas that deals with the occult. But in 'autobiographical' works she often writes about it. In *The Pure and the Impure* she discusses a case of jealousy. Another woman and herself were both in love with the same man (Jouvenel, presumably). Colette almost died of various accidents at the time, till she felt that an evil will was at work, and she concentrated against it. The bad spell passed, and when she met the woman, years later, and they became friends, the woman confessed she had actively wished Colette dead in the very period in which the 'accidents' were occurring. Was the memory of Délia – if she ever existed – revived in Colette's mind in the late 1930s by the fact that Willy had died in 1931, Jouvenel in 1935? Was she pondering the relation between those deaths and her actual writing? For she had 'dealt' with Willy in *My Apprenticeships*, and with Jouvenel in *Julie de Carneilhan*. The lady was great, but not what you could call nice. There had also been *La Seconde*, and *Duo* . . . with Michel's suicide, and Alice's survival. Might it not be the case that, in *Rainy Moon*, Colette is not just showing that there can be evil in the midst of the most mundane and cosy situation, that the typist's sister or the chemist's wife may be primitive murderesses, but, more importantly, giving birth to (as well as repudiating) her own black double? Délia is the narrator's evil reincarnation, the person she might or may have been – there is no telling, since only diffracted light, diffracted time, a casual encounter, chance involuntary memory, enable that dimension of the self to be perceived. Fortune-tellers whom the narrator visits leave her shipwrecked amidst the welter of the past and promises of a distant future:

> . . . the temptation persists, along with a definite itch . . . to climb three floors or work a shaky lift, stop on a landing and ring three times. You see, one day, I might hear my own

footsteps approaching on the other side of the door and my own voice asking me rudely: 'What is it?' I open the door to myself and, naturally, I am wearing what I used to wear in the old days.... The bitch I had in 1900 puts up her hackles and shivers when she sees me double.... The end is missing. But as good nightmares go, it's a good nightmare. (*SC:* 161)

Here Madame Colette goes in, confronts Délia, sits on her bed, rocks her in her arms as, in 1907, in *The Tendrils of the Vine*, 'Colette Willy' had sat on her own sofa with Claudine, her creation, her haunting double. As she had been rocked in Missy's arms. The narrator/protagonist feels indulgent to Délia, tender. She is alarmed by her. Lying silent across the dark entrance, Délia is ominous. It was Eugène she hoped had rung. Witchcraft means that he would have made his own death certain if he had trodden over her. It is the narrator who almost does. Thus a strange ambiguity is created. Like Prince Charming, the almost masculine protagonist forces gradual entry into the recesses of the apartment where Délia/Sleeping Beauty/her own past self, confined to bed by a spell that has sharp things in it (not a distaff, but plenty of sharp needles), lies. As such, she might be a substitute for Eugène – might be killed in his place? She has a vigorous, 'masculine' reaction catching the oblique glance that filters towards her through the thick eyelashes, she slaps Délia hard, who comes to straight-away, cross, reduced to the status of a shamming child. Yet Madame Colette *feeds* Délia: buys cherries for her from the merchant's cart in the street, as for a child. The last time she catches sight of the new widow, Délia is eating chips from a paper bag, like a kid. Is the protagonist feeding the murderess in herself? Her own potential daughter? She, as retrospective narrator, owns up to her then frustrated maternal feelings, her need to cuddle and fondle and spoil.

Whatever the answer, a veritable prism of forces become arrayed. In the process, those three figures, so well identified by Catherine Clément,[3] the witch, the hysteric, the whore, are completely rehauled. White witches come to the rescue, to free the narrator from her seductive double: for there is something of what Freud has described as the 'uncanny' in that otherwise so homely story; the protagonist stumbles over a kind of predatory oval protrait, a new Ligeia. The excursion with Annie de Pène, the lore of the groom at the studs, Sido's visit, help Colette forget about the two sisters. Sido brings a token of white magic which, like rainy moon, has to do with the weather: an ear of oats with barometric properties, which rotates according to whether it is going to rain or be fine. There is a pun in the French on 'temps', time, but also weather. Sido's oats rotate like a beneficent little needle, it forms a circle as Sido, from her house and garden in Saint-Sauveur, was at the centre of a 'rose des vents' whose concentric circles expanded beyond the village and woods. Sido brings roses in a wet towel, there are a dozen roses in the narrator's flat. Sido could tell what the weather was going to be like, she could read the portents. Her circles were centred, petals of a flower, a living matrix, a magic lantern in her daughter's imagination. Rainy moon diffracts.

If Sido could read the weather, the protagonist has trouble reading the signs that the Barberet sisters present her with. She has particular trouble interpreting Délia's face, though it is a childish face, and she has a keen eye for the signs that can betray a child's secret intent. What the Inquisition did with witches and doctors with hysterics, the protagonist does to the people who confront her (and you could say that Délia is a witch and shams hysterical symptoms, as when she's supposed to have passed out right across the entrance). She is attracted to the *asymmetrical*, the 'odd' (Poe's term, translated by Baudelaire as 'le bizarre'). It was odd signs and marks that Inquisitors and doctors looked for on the bodies of witches or hysterics. The narrator/protagonist, however, is aware of ulterior motives and, after all, using an appropriate novelistic craft. That does not make it easy for her to interpret those odd signs that draw her. In *Bella-Vista*, she begins to warm up to Mr Daste when he displays a bruise on one side of his face, the mark of a night-bird's sharp beak: it humanizes his face for her. But it turns out that Mr Daste has a perverse relish for killing birds, which ends up nauseating her as Délia's black practices, expounded by Rosita, finally nauseate her. In *Rainy Moon*, asymmetricality can be so complex as to be overwhelming, when it spreads its prism. It is when Rosita begins to go to pieces, because her sister's spell is working, that she ceases to look well-kempt: her ringlets, the two little 'sausages' so decorously laid next to each other, disappear, replaced by an old-maidish, straggly bun. Yet she becomes most human when, drunk on *Lunel* wine, turned into a kind of *lunatic*, her hair half-undone and *one* cheek flushed, she tells the narrator all about Délia – and a few home-truths to boot.

There are other 'good' witches than Sido, other dealers in portents. During her nightly beat with her cat, the local prostitute, a country lass who has nothing to do with traditional representations of the whore, exchanges a few words with the protagonist. On the night of Rosita's visit, she announces that the weather is about to change: '"the mist is all in one long sheet over the stream"' (*SC*: 200). She appears to the narrator as a guardian presence, 'with her shadow crouched at her feet, this shepherdess without a flock who... thought of the Seine as a stream'. Kindly too, and with a gift for seeing the future is Marie Mallier, a seamstress who sews for pleasure; so are the 'ten or twenty francs' sibyls' the narrator/protagonist normally frequents, who 'touch hands' round a dinner table and 'converse with the great beyond' in a state of gentle, benevolent innocence (*SC*: 169, 197). On the other side are arrayed black or purple figures. Like Marie Mallier, Délia is a seamstress. Her long sharp needles seem to be embroidering an elaborate pattern for a purse (no need to go into Freudian explanations here any more than for the staircase). She is in effect stitching a bad spell. Things get worse, or so Rosita intimates, when sharp scissors come into play, and the needles get dipped into a nauseating substance. But Rosita herself, is she not caught in the same web? And the narrator/protagonist/ author? They have needles too. The typist types in black, makes black or purple copies. She uses the prongs of her typewriters on the scripts the protagonist brings her: signs that the narrator/protagonist has made with her prong or needle of a pen ... Making copies, the typist makes the scripts double. She points out that in the script p. 7, by mistake, follows p. 3. Seven colours of the rainbow, seven moons for Délia to kill Eugène, three fatal sisters ... Délia compares the concentration that she requires to do her mysterious task to that required by the novelist. She calls it a 'profession', 'a bit like a novel, only better' (*SC*: 185). The narrator, at any rate pulls out, feeling that she does 'not care for the picturesque, when it is based on ... black hatred' (197). She discards the pieces she's written and that Rosita has typed, she ceases to go to the Barberets'. She tries to stop being the third sister. (Who is Atropos, the one with the sharp scissors? Délia?) But her conscious withdrawal, her erasure of her own text, do not prevent Eugène's death from happening. At the end of the story, Délia (the carbon copy?) is in black, or purple, mourning.

When Colette writes the story, Sido is dead, Annie de Pène is dead, Willy, Jouvenel and Missy are dead.

Rainy Moon makes it impossible to answer the questions I've asked. It is even a simplification to say, as I have done, that there are 'white' or 'black' witches: there is an impenetrable and touching childishness about Délia, for instance. What there is, is prismatic witch-craft, a number of ways of reading or projecting patterns, among which the signs of writing themselves are caught. The author/narrator confesses that she lacks the 'unbridled imagination' that would pluck out of events their poetic, their 'catastrophic truth'. She is grounded in herself, intent on the differences 'between what really happens and what does not ... between an event and the narration of it'. And so she cannot slough her skin and emerge 'in new, variegated colours' thanks to such episodes as that in *Rainy Moon*, which yet was a little 'present' fate had offered her: another writer would have taken off at full gallop (170). In this sense too *Rainy Moon* is a blank. The little rainbow globe, the sign and portent, keeps closing its one, its odd eye: its eyelid is white, or barely patterned, like the wallpaper. Yet throughout the story it has shone, making it impossible to tell where autobiography begins and fiction ends, but giving the whole thing an air of extraordinary reality, showing the multiple folds of the self, caught up in the diffracted or rose-window lights of its past. The one certainty is that white (the blank which is the story, the story in which you could say that nothing, indeed, happens to the narrator, not even writing since that is destroyed) is the colour that is produced when the colours of the prism rotate fast enough.

It is also the colour of the crêpe band under Délia's chin.

Conclusion: Fever and Flight

'I went towards flight as towards a liberation, towards a
light.' (Genêt, *The Miracle of the Rose*)

'To fly is the gesture of woman, to fly in language, to make
it fly.'

(Hélène Cixous, *La Jeune Née*, 1975: 178)

For Christiane Veschambre, to whose essay on Colette,
'Affections de la langue-mère', I owe so much.

'My trouble with Colette,' I confided to a friend as I was
beginning to work on this book, 'is that I don't know if
I'm enough like her, and if I like her enough, to travel
such a long way with her. I'm not that keen on animals,
apart from birds – and she's got such vitality, such
sensuous bounce. She doesn't seem to know about feeling
low – about illness, grief, what's called the darker side of
life.' 'Perhaps you haven't read enough of her work,' my
friend replied. 'Or perhaps you haven't been *reading* her.'
She was right. From that early period in Paris as Willy's

200

wife, when she was so ill she would have died if Sido hadn't come and nursed her back to health, Colette knows misery, remembers that she's flown close to the crystal doors. But she conceals her knowledge and her memory under what in other times would have been called stoicism, aristocratic restraint. Pastel clouds of spleen, and some slate-coloured, drift through *The Tendrils of the Vine, The Vagabond, The Shackle*. Heart-pangs so acute they affect her as a fever make Léa take to her bed. With the autobiographies, grief at the loss of the childhood, the childhood village, the mother, struggling with the need to renounce, the memories of the 'prisons' of her 'apprenticeships', strike vibrant chords. But from June 1940 onwards, multiplied sources of pain flow into Colette's life. She lives through the defeat, the exodus. Maurice Goudeket is arrested and put in a camp in Compiègne. Colette manages to get him released, but he spends the rest of the war in fear and in hiding, and the sound of the tinkling door bell the morning the soldiers came for Maurice shakes something out of Colette, that never comes back. And gradually, she becomes paralysed by arthritis. Her last years are spent in pain, on the 'raft' of the chaise-longue on the second floor of her Palais-Royal apartment.

Colette meets the shocks (June 1940, and those that followed) as French peasants (as she reminds herself and her reader), through centuries of invasions, have met the Eastern hordes that trampled their harvests and occupied their homes – but who, one day, were gone (*JR*: 8). Sido, confronted in 1870 with her first Prussian soldier, a grey shadow one grey dawn in the mist that rose from a neighbouring spring, rushed back home to protect her children and bury her best wine in the cellar sand. Colette also stores the forces of life. She works at cheerfulness. She looks into the grey mist, her mother's verbal memory of that dramatic dawn, and it becomes a mirror blurred by her mother's breath, out of which her own words and visions will rise. She keeps going. She keeps writing. That is what she can do. All her roads lead to a table: a writing-table. In the sand she shakes from her hands to dry the writing after she's written, 'the end', she sees the words 'à suivre': 'to be continued'. When the end is even nearer, in *The Blue Lantern*, she rejoices that her fading senses only show that she's drifting away on that raft of hers, not that the world is diminishing in any way. Oh that more writers, instead of making their own sense of an ending into an apocalypse, were capable of such modest generosity:

> Instead of reaching islands, am I then sailing towards the open sea, where I only hear the solitary sound of my heart, like the sound of the surf? Nothing is perishing, I'm the one who is drifting away, let us take heart. The open sea, but not the desert. To discover that there is no desert: it is enough for me to conquer what besets me. (*FB*: 8)

And she is game. For anything life is still willing to dangle in front of her nose:

> I am lucky, then, to have pain, which I reconcile with a gambler's spirit, my ultra-feminine gambler's spirit, my taste for play, if you prefer it: the Last Cat, as she was dying, showed by the movement of her paw, by the smile on her face, that a trailing piece of string was still for her a plaything, food for feline thought and illusion. Those who surround me will not let me want for pieces of string. (*FB*: 12)

But intense pain also forces Colette to concentrate, write (however randomly it may seem) at a pitch she's never kept to before. She evokes a friend who liked *The*

Break of Day best of all her books, and regretted she didn't write more like it. 'Don't you think "idées fixes" are horrible?' she asked him. 'Not so,' he said. He'd lived all his life with one – lived in constant pain from a lame leg. That, of course, is a particular kind of 'idée fixe'. In Colette, arthritic pain acts as an intensive and almost continuous involuntary memory in the late years. It flares up: it is a trail of fire that illuminates the past in the suffering body. It brings back the illness in early married life, and the motherly presence that is part and parcel of a child's illness. The bond goes both ways: it is with the mother, in the story 'The Sick Child'. With the daughter, in 'La Fièvre'.

Fever creates that wild imaginative gallop that the narrator of 'Rainy Moon' claimed she couldn't take. It provides an entry into what others call the absolute. A pagan, an agnostic, an amoralist, Colette? No. One whose faith in life is boundless, she has looked into 'the Great Beyond', and decided she'd keep her distance. She would not betray the mother who wanted her to keep on living. Not for her the archetypal equation of Death and The Mother. But she knew the temptation. The temptation to go mad, the temptation to die.

There are two versions of this temptation. In 'La Fièvre', fever overtakes the narrator of *Looking Backwards* while Maurice and herself, Colette, have sought refuge in Bel-Gazou's derelict castle, at the end of June 1940. Fever despatches to her, as she tries to get up to collect her scattered blue papers, 'one of its best-winged vertigoes',

> a major Vertigo that has swooped down on the strewn leaves at the same time as myself. But to get there first, it knocked me hard on the head with its feathered shoulder. (*JR*: 43)

As she abdicates, she, a-political Colette, has a vision of a blond, awkward young man, the King of Belgium, listening to the imagined sound of his crown rolling away from him on its edge like the metal circle of a barrel... Shivering, she goes to bed, begins to write: 'A writer seized by fever remains a writer. For a few hours even, s/he is an improved writer... Thanks to the fever, it is Sunday every minute...'. Should she always write under its burning aegis? (*JR*: 45). Fever blows great 'vvvou's around her, with a profusion of 'v's. It seems to have borrowed all the 'v's of large airy words like 'vent, vortex, vol'. Wind, vortex, flight. In *The Evening Star*, the star *V*enus will also fly through the night on its 'v's and 'f's, since it is called *V*esper at sunset, *V*enus at night and Luci*f*er at dawn. But 'La Fièvre' gives Colette double sight. She can guess what is going on on the other side of the partition, beyond the walls of the house, far away... And a shadow, a strange shadow, joins her.

The shadow of a child. A little girl. It gave me quite a shock, reading that passage. I almost wrote the same scene myself, in my novel *L'Entremise*. There the little girl turned nasty, drew near. She does not, in Colette. She is a known visitor, with long flat hair, a blue dress, yellow button boots. She comes forward just so far, and no further. Looks over the gate erected by Colette, who will not let her past. 'One has the apparitions one deserves.' 'If, seeing a wolf in the place of her Grandmother, little Red Riding Hood had simply passed on, the Wolf would never have existed.' Confronted with uncanny visitors or reputedly dangerous animals, the thing to do is not to raise your voice. Keep cool. Otherwise the apparition will devour you. Thus Colette resists the temptation to let the illusory fish she keeps hallucinating in the jug of water by her bedside, become a fish. 'Ingenuous grub... you'll have to go hungry. You are dealing with a Red

Riding Hood that could eat you up as fried gudgeon.' The little girl, over there, knows she is allowed to look, but not to touch. Colette won't let her come near for the same reason that she never yielded to the siren calls of death.

> She comes from far away. In the hours of fever, Sido my mother used to lean over me: 'Do you want a drink, Minet-Chéri?' Above all else I wanted her not to catch sight of my suspect twin, the flat-haired little girl she might have loved. (*JR*: 51)

Sido came to Paris to nurse her fever-stricken daughter at the time when Freud was writing *Traumdeutung*. He relates how a father dreamt of his dead son. There is a fire. The child calls out, 'Father, can't you see that I am burning?' No one – Lacan comments – can say what the death of a child is, except the father as Father – 'that is, no *conscious* being'.[1]

Some fathers have tried. Mallarmé, for instance, grieving over his dead son, and erecting his tomb in 'Pour un tombeau d'Anatole'. The text perhaps proves Lacan's point. Colette did elaborate the theme of fever, coming close to death, many times from *Claudine in Paris* onwards, and more especially in the late texts. But in her texts, there is always water. The jug of water, in 'La Fièvre'. Sido saying, 'Do you want a drink, Minet-Chéri?' Sido had given her adolescent daughter the two secret springs, the one that tasted of the stem of hyacinths and the one that tasted of iron and oak-leaves. The taste that she knew would be with her when she finally went. 'Une source, c'est toujours un miracle.' 'A spring is always a miracle.' To Freud's and Lacan's 'Father, can't you see that I am burning?', she answers with a 'Child, do you want a drink?' Or indeed, to daughter Bel-Gazou who longs to know love she says, 'Child, I promise you that you will burn.' She turns the patriarchal questions and answers round, she refuses the fascination for death. As once already, to the child in Freud suffering from the mother's absence in his game of 'fort/da', she had answered with the mother missing the hidden children, her echoing call, 'Where are the children?'

'A child is burning.' In a sense, Lacan is right. Illness is one of the great rites of passage of the nineteenth-century imagination, and an experience that is never told, that remains a blank in the text. Marianne Dashwood in *Sense and Sensibility*, Pip, Esther Summerson, Mr Rochester, Caroline Helstone, many others, and Claudine herself in *Claudine in Paris*, sail close to death. The trip enables them to change, mature, expiate, adapt, leave behind another self. But what goes on to effect such a change, what the fever is, never gets written from the point of view of the sufferer. Colette calmly inhabits that territory. Perhaps because she herself had come so close to dying when she was young, perhaps because she had recreated the bond-in-writing with the mother's body, the body that watches over the child's illness: and so she was both the sick child, and the loving watcher, the one who had the experience, and the one who could contain it in language.

Fever, for Colette, is associated more and more with flight. 'Vol', the soaring 'v's, 'fièvre', 'vertige', 'vortex'. Magically, in those moments in which consciousness is lost, which only those who have crossed madness, flipped, tripped, have written about and tried to charter, Colette or the boy in the magnificent late story 'The Sick Child', pass into a state of levitation, of joy, which is close to what in religious terms is called paradise. Robert Cottrell, in the main a sensitive critic of Colette, claims however that Colette has no sense of verticality, that even the woods in Claudine's beloved Montigny are somehow horizontal.[2] He had forgotten how birds appear more and more frequently in her work, from the nightingale of *The Tendrils of the Vine* through the pigeons and 'chats-huants' of *Bella-Vista* and the owls of *La Paix chez les bêtes*, and how little Jean (alias Colette when she was a child and a young woman alias Colette the old woman now nailed to her raft by arthritis) can ride the objects round the room, and, Peter Pan-like, fly through the window into pure space.

Interesting that he should be called Jean, the little boy paralysed by poliomyelitis, spoiled by Madam Mamma and the servant Mandora with the golden name. Jean, like Jean Genêt, Christiane Veschambre points out: Jean Genêt alone has the art of writing such weightless, levitating sentences. One of the few male writers in whom Hélène Cixous says she's found 'feminine' sentences.[3] More immediately for Colette, for she died too soon to know Genêt, Jean like Jean Giono, the golden-haired young writer she liked, or like Jean Marais, also golden-haired, who was playing Chéri at the theatre and kept visiting her. Jean, also, like the lover in *The Shackle*, the lover who reveals to Renée the fullness of adult passion.

In 'The Sick Child', the 'semiotic' and the 'symbolic' combine in the most aerial way. Like the child, who rides clouds of fragrance through the house and beyond the house, the writer rides language into imaginative freedom, but with perfect horse(wo)manship. Sounds tremble into other possibilities. What had been revealed to the healthy child through the word 'presbytery' is a continuous experience for the sick child: Antonia White, the translator, has done a very good job of an almost impossible task:

The shearer of golden fleece, the river and the meadow faded away like a dream, leaving behind on Jean's forehead a sweet, commonplace scent and a wavy crest of fair hair. Jean, waking up, heard a whispering coming from the drawing-room, a long low colloquy between Madam Mamma and the doctor from which one word escaped, crisp and lively, and made a beeline for Jean, the word 'crisis'. Sometimes it entered ceremoniously, like a lady dressed up to give away prizes, with an *h* behind its ear and a *y* tucked into its bodice: Chrysis, Chrysis Wilby-Sallatry. 'Truly? Truly?' said the urgent voice of Madam Mamma. 'I said: perhaps...' replied the doctor's voice, an unsteady voice that halted on one foot. 'A crisis, salutary but severe...' Chrysis Salutari Sevea, a young creole from tropical America, lissom in her flounced white cotton dress.

The child's subtle ear also gathered the name of another person which no doubt it was expedient to keep secret. A name he couldn't quite catch, something like Polly O'Miley or Olly O'Miall and he finally decided it must refer to some little girl, also stricken with painful immobility and possessed of two long useless legs, whom they never mentioned in front of him in case he should be jealous. (*SC:* 355)

Jean flies very close to death. He cannot cry, 'to the rescue, Madam Mamma!' Confronted with somebody more powerful than his mother, not a little girl who could be told not to come one step nearer, nor a seducer dressed in taffeta, but still an adversary of Madam Mamma, one who has the power to keep her anxiously waiting on the other side of the wall and imposes silence with a 'haughty sign', he bravely forbears to call for help:

So he did not scream. In any case, the unknown beings, the fabulous strangers, were already beginning to abduct him by force. Rising up on all sides, they poured burning heat and icy cold on him, racked him with melodious torture,

swathed him in colour like a bandage, swung him in a
hammock of palpitations. With his face already turned to
flee, motionless, to his mother, he suddenly changed his
mind and launched himself in full flight, letting his own
impetus carry him where it would, through meteors and
mists and lightnings that softly opened to let him through,
closed behind him, opened again ... And, just as he was on
the very verge of being perfectly content, ungrateful and
gay, exulting in his solitude as an only child, his privileges as
an orphan and an invalid, he was aware that a sad little
crystalline crash separated him from a bliss whose
beautiful, soft, airy name he had yet to learn: death. A little,
light melancholy crash, coming perhaps from some planet
deserted for ever ... The clear and sorrowful sound,
clinging to the child who was going to die, held on so
staunchly that the dazzling escape tried in vain to shake it
off and outdistance it. (SC: 358–9)

But Jean survives. As he survives, he loses the power
of magic that the fever had given him:

He sat up without assistance in bed, towing his still-heavy
legs that were overrun with ants. In the depths of the
window, in the celestial waters of night swam the curved
moon and the dim reflection of a long-haired child, to whom
he beckoned. He raised one arm, and the other child
obediently copied his summoning gesture. Slightly intoxicated with the power to work marvels, he called up his boon
companions of the cruel but privileged hours; the visible
sounds; the tangible images; the breathable seas; the
nourishing, navigable air; the wings that mocked feet; the
laughing suns.

... Then he waited, but nothing came. Nothing came that
night or the following ones, nothing ever again.

... Was it possible that the damask alp, piled high in the
big cupboard, would henceforth refuse to allow a child who
was nearly well to perform the feats a small cripple had
achieved on the slopes of imaginary glaciers?

... A time comes when one is forced to concentrate on living. A time comes when one has to renounce dying in full flight. With a wave of his hand, Jean said farewell to his angel-haired reflection. The other returned his greeting from the depths of an earthly night shorn of all marvels, the only night allowed to children whom death lets go and who fall asleep, assenting, cured and disappointed. (SC: 366-7)

And this is where Colette leaves us. On the one side, there is living, the springs whose savoury waters are ever accessible, the renewed marvel of taste and smell and sound and sight. On the other, the other marvel, the full flight of the sick child, expanding to infinite space, the sky in which Vesper shines, the open sea towards which the ageing woman is gamefully drifting. Sido's rose of the winds, expanded and made into writing by her daughter, deserves the name that the other Jean was going to use for one of his books, also about 'vol': *The Miracle of the Rose.*

Notes

PART I

Chapter 1: The Domestic Circle
1. In an extremely interesting paper that she had the kindness to show me, ('Biography and Identification', MLA conference 1984), Elaine Marks deals with this in helpful and suggestive detail. She proposes that 'the possibility of identification between reader and biographee [is] the major reason why the alliance between the biographical enquiry and the feminist enquiry has been so strong'. She uses 'identification' in the Freudian sense and claims that a danger lies there, since the identification is occurring 'precisely at the moment when the biographical enquiry is being labelled as epistemologically naive'.

Chapter 2: Phynance
1. To Antole de Monzie, end February 1924.
2. In François Caradec, *Feu Willy: avec et sans Colette*, 1984. Also see Paul d'Hollander, *Colette: ses apprentissages*, 1978, and his wonderfully full notes to the first volume of the Pléiade edition of Colette.
3. Obviously Colette's story is only one side of the story, though the major one. For corrections as to dates and

211

details and a more 'objective' reconstitution of events, see the books quoted above.

4. Which various biographers have tried to do: Sylvain Bonmariage wrote a poison account of Colette. For interestingly mixed views, see again the books above and Geneviève Dormann who champions Willy in her *Amoureuse Colette*, 1984.

Chapter 3: The Name of the Father I

1. Antoinette Fouque, 'Culture des femmes: Une gestation', in *Des femmes en mouvement hebdo*, Nos. 53–54, August 1981.
2. See Engels on Morgan in *The Origins of the Family*, 1972 and the multiple debates that have flown from it. I very much like Séverine Auffret's speculations in her book on excision, *Des Couteaux contre des femmes*, 1983; and in *Nous, Clytemnestre*, 1985.
3. See Hélène Cixous, 'The Laugh of the Medusa', in Marks and De Courtivron, *New French Feminisms*, 1981: 245–64.
4. Joanna Richardson, *Colette*, 1983. The biographer makes great and, in my opinion, insufficiently critical use of the two stepsons' 'revelation's and in particular of Renaud's, a hostile witness.

Chapter 4: My Father's Daughter

1. What Sido disapproved of was her children getting *married*, not having their affairs. She is wonderfully ironic about traditional moral views of marriage. Thus in a late letter to Colette who is in the thick of her passion for Jouvenel, Sido writes, 'Can you thus wallow in the delights of Capua? Did I ever do that? Yes,' (with Captain Colette) 'but then, as I got married, *the sin was removed from it.*' Colette/Sido, *Lettres*, 1984: 449. The reference is to Agnès, in *L'Ecole des femmes*, who is told by her tutor Arnolphe that the only way to remove the 'crime' of pleasure is to get married.
2. 'Notre pays, notre terre de naissance, c'est le corps maternel, et c'est un corps de femme: Entretien avec Antoinette Fouque', *Des femmes en mouvement*, mai 1982, No. 1: 10–14.

Chapter 5: The Name of the Father II

1. See Paul d'Hollander (1978: 55–63) and Claude Pichois's Preface to Colette: *Oeuvres* (1984: x–cxxii) as well as

François Caradec.

2. In his use of his grandmother's surname, you could say that Willy created a model for Céline. His pen-surname is his grandmother's first name. As for playing with 'willy', D.H. Lawrence comes a close second with the Willey Waters of *Women in Love*.

3. See James' Preface to *The Awkward Age*, 1899.

4. Julia Kristéva (1977 and 1981).

5. To feel how totally weird all that name-playing is, let us speculate on the equivalent happening to Mrs Thatcher. Let us imagine that her maiden name had been Margaret Penny, and that Mr Thatcher was a writer whose grandmother had been called Keswick. To his double-barrel name of Thatcher-Keswick he would have substituted the pen-name of Quéquette (the French equivalent of 'willy'). He would also have called his wife by her surname of Penny. And when Margaret Penny, now Margaret Thatcher, had become an author herself, Mr Thatcher would have signed her books 'Quéquette'. Later, when she had become independent, she would have used the pen-name of Penny Quéquette.

6. *Gil Blas*, 4 June 1904, quoted by Claude Pichois.

7. Startlingly, the old catalogue of Cambridge University Library refers all entries on Colette to H. Gauthier-Villars (Madame). The implications are clear...

PART II

Chapter 6: Figures of Love and Desire

1. Lélia rejects her suitor's romantic grandiloquence. 'Man, do not seek for hell nor for heaven in me,' she pleads. 'Do not seek for such deep mysteries. My soul is the sister of yours, it knows grief and joy like you.' Colette's Alice, in *Duo*, is exasperated that men should assume that women's desires are necessarily different from their own; that women cannot simply know lust like themselves (*Duo:* 53–4).

2. See in particular Cixous/Clément, *La Jeune née*, 1975; and Bernheimer/Kahane (eds.), *In Dora's Case*, 1985.

3. Malinowski, *The Ethnography of – The Trobriand Islands*, 1979.

4. My mother has reconstituted various branches of our

family tree. Ours is a wide ranging 'middle'-class family, going from the milliner to the fashion-designer, the labourer and barrel-maker and Napoleonic soldier to the cardinal. In the nineteenth century and turn of the century, several times, a niece marries her uncle. One of the results, interestingly, is that you get several women with the same name. You wonder which 'Rose Jouve' you are dealing with – as you do, which Colette.

5. See *Homosexualities in French Literature*, 1974, in particular I. de Courtivron's article on George Sand, 'Weak Men and Fatal Women'.

6. Things are different when a woman writes. Thus when George Sand creates the love of Lélia and Pulchérie for each other, the stress is upon a sisterly community of experience, and tenderness.

7. Quotation and following discussion are from pp. 8–9 of Catherine van Casselaer's very informative and sprightly *Lot's Wife, Lesbian Paris, 1890–1914: 1986*. The documentation of lesbians in Paris that I go on to produce owes much to this book, as well as to Paul d'Hollander, Claude Pichois, Parker and Pollock's *Old Mistresses: Women, Art and Ideology* (their discussion of Rosa Bonheur), Jean Chalon's life of Natalie Clifford-Barney, *Portrait d'une séductrice*, 1976 and Natalie's own *Souvenirs indiscrets*.

8. *Lot's Wife*, op. cit., 44.

9. Id., 77.

10. Yvonne Mitchell was the first biographer to produce detailed evidence about Missy.

11. Adrienne Rich, *On Lies, Secrets and Silence: Selected Prose*, 1980, 200.

12. Lilian Federman, *Surpassing the Love of Men: Romantic Friendship and Love between Women from the Renaissance to the Present*, 1981: 363.

13. For a thought-provoking analysis of 'representation' see Susan Kappeler, *The Pornography of Representation*, 1985, as well as controversies arising from Lacan's *Encore*, well-summarized in Stephen Heath, 'Difference', *Screen*, XIX 1978: 51–112.

14. Quoted, and commented upon, by J.H. Stewart, *Colette*, 1983: 48–9.

15. Lawrence asks the same question as Freud & Co. in *Women in Love*, and offers a very different answer to Colette's:

What was it, after all, that a woman wanted? Was it mere social effect, fulfilment of ambition in the social world, in the community of mankind? Was it even a union in love and goodness? Did she want 'goodness'? . . .

What then, what next? Was it sheer blind force of passion that would satisfy her now? Not this, but the subtle thrills of extreme sensation in reduction . . .

But between two particular people, any two people on earth, the range of pure sensational experience is limited. The climax of sensual reaction, once reached in any direction, is reached finally, there is no going on. There is only repetition possible, or the going apart of the two protagonists, or the subjugating of the one will to the other, or death.

. . . The world was finished now, for her. There was only the inner, individual darkness, sensation within the ego, the obscene religious mystery of ultimate reduction, the mystic frictional activities of diabolic reducing down, disintegrating the vital organic body of life.

All this Gudrun knew in her subconsciousness, . . . (Penguin Books, 1985: 507–8)

Chapter 7: The Mother's Houses

1. Sido's letters are evidence of this, and so are *Sido* and *The Break of Day*.
2. Colette talked about the nightingales in front of the abbé Mugnier, who recounts it in his diaries. My father sent me the extract, mixing his own memories of Fez with it.
3. In a letter Sido tells Colette that they are both at least three centuries ahead of their time: they both attach importance to what, to others, are the 'little nothings' of life. On this attention to the seemingly unimportant, see Elaine Marks, *Colette*, 1960: 224.
4. 'Why Molly Bloom menstruates', in Richard Ellmann, *Ulysses On The Liffey*, 1972: 159 onwards. My thanks to Rebecca Stott for revealing this passage to me at a crucial stage in my thinking about the four cardinal points in Colette.

PART III

Chapter 8: The Mother Tongue

1. Julia Kristéva, 'From One Identity to An Other', *Desire In Language*, 1980: 136ff. See also S. Relyea and Nancy K. Miller's essays in Eisinger/McCarthy, 1981.
2. Editions des femmes, 1985.
3. One of them, Bizoute, is away, and never returns in either novel. I have heard Antoinette Fouque argue that three are always four but that the fourth one if hidden, is perhaps the 'placenta'. The three musketeers are four, the Brontë sisters are four children/authors, the brother (Branwell) being the fourth. Strikingly, in *Le Toutounier*, the three sisters are also four.

Chapter 9: Currencies

1. On the letter see in particular Ruth Perry, *Women, Letters and the Novel*, 1980. Also J.H. Stewart, 'Colette and the Epistolary Novel', In Eisinger/McCarthy, 1981. J. Giry, *Colette et l'art du discours intérieur*, 1981: 195–6. A complex set of connections are suggested between love, letters (in both senses of the word), mysticism, the soul in Lacan's 'Une lettre d'amour', Séminaire XX *Encore*, 1975.
2. Claudine Hermann, *Les Voleuses de langue*, 1976: 58–65, 99–135.
3. Rewriting this, I have become aware of how close this is to Hélène Cixous's *La Venue à l'écriture*, 1977. On Colette and age, see S. Tinter, 1980.
4. *Mémoires d'une jeune fille rangée*, 1958: 77.
5. The Antonia White translation runs as follows: 'Only Madame Suzanne's bust was visible. Every time the kitchen hatch opened, her golden hair and her hot face appeared in its frame against a background of shining saucepans and gridirons' (*SC*: 14). I must note again how much can be lost even by an excellent translator.

Chapter 10: De-fetishizing Writing

1. As the abbé Mugnier, a witty witness to the high-brow literary life of the 1920s and 1930s, reports in his journal, and as many other witnesses confirm.
2. Letter to Marguerite Moréno, quoted in M. Crosland, *Colette, The Difficulty of Loving*, 1973: 142.

3. 'Green Wax', *CS:* 304.

Chapter 11: Autobiography as Prism
1. Philippe Lejeune, *Le Pacte autobiographique*, 1975.
2. See Donna Norell, 'The Relationship between Meaning and Structure in Colette's *Rain-Moon'*, in Eisinger/McCarthy, 1981: 54–65. She makes perceptive points about the way names, colours and numbers function.
3. Cixous/Clément, *La Jeune née*, 1975, 'Sorcière et hystérique', 9–78. The whole essay could be applied in detail to 'Rainy Moon' in all sorts of ways.

CONCLUSION: FEVER AND FLIGHT

1. J. Lacan, Séminaire Livre XI, *Les Quatre concepts fondamentaux de la Psychanalyse*, 1973: 55–9.
2. Robert Cottrell, *Colette,* 1974: 17.
3. Christiane Veschambre, 'Affections de la langue-mère', *Land* 5/6, 1983: 23–31. Also Hélène Cixous, 'The Laughter of the Medusa', *op. cit.*

Selected Bibliography

The Works of Colette

I Collected Works

Colette herself prepared an edition of her works which included a bibliography in the last volume. It appeared as *Oeuvres complètes de Colette*, 15 vols., Paris, Flammarion (Le Fleuron): 1948–50. A re-edition (including some posthumous pieces) came out for the centenary of her birth (1873), in 16 illustrated volumes: Editions du Club de l'Honnête Homme, 1973–76. Since then, however, Flammarion have brought out a new three-volume edition, *Oeuvres*, 1984. The same year, the first volume of what is to be *Oeuvres* (excluding music, theatre and cinema criticism but including everything else), came out (Gallimard, Pléiade, 1984; other volumes to follow). It is certain to become the standard edition, as it includes, beside excellent introductions, variants and notes, a detailed chronology and a complete bibliography (for vol. I, up to 1983 for works up to 1910). As the editors point out, the *Oeuvres complètes* are not in effect 'complete', as there were hundreds of articles Colette had not at hand (lost or forgotten in removals...) when the Flammarion edition was prepared. There are no *Collected Works* of Colette in English.

Selected Bibliography

II Separate works in order in publication

For bibliographies of Colette's works, see the Pléiade edition for up to 1910; for later periods, consult the bibliography in the *Oeuvres complètes* as well as Paul d'Hollander, 1978 and Michèle Sarde, 1978 and 1981. For a bibliography of Colette in translation, see Margery Resnick and Isabelle de Courtivron, *Women Writers in Translation, An Annotated Bibliography*, New York and London, Garland Publishing, Inc., 1984. Also Eleanor Reid Gibbard, 'A Chronology of Colette in English Translation', *West Virginia University Philological Papers 23*, no. 7-1 (Jan. 1977): 75-93.

Basically, the history of Colette in English is a headache: some works have not been translated, others have appeared in several different translations as well as in different editions both in England and the USA. Some works have been cut, regrouped, etc., and to cap it all, others are in and out of print like a yoyo. I have only included here the most readily available translations in England. For translations in the US, see the bibliographies above as well as Joan Stewart Hinde's *Colette*, 1983. Farrar, Straus and Giroux are the main publisher of Colette (New York) in the US.

(All editions published in Paris or London unless otherwise indicated.)

Claudine à l'école, Ollendorff, 1900. *Claudine At School*, Secker and Warburg, 1956.

Claudine à Paris, Ollendorff, 1901. *Claudine in Paris*, Secker and Warburg, 1958; Penguin Books, 1972.

Claudine amoureuse, Ollendorff, 1902. *Claudine en ménage*, Mercure de France, 1902. *Claudine Married*, Secker and Warburg, 1960; Penguin Books, 1972.

Claudine s'en va, Ollendorff, 1903. *Claudine and Annie*, Secker and Warburg, 1962; Penguin Books, 1963, 1972.

Minne, Ollendorff, 1904.

Dialogues de bêtes, Mercure de France, 1904. *Creature Conversations* in *Creatures Great and Small*, Secker and Warburg, 1951.

Les Egarements de Minne, Ollendorff, 1905.

Sept Dialogues de bêtes. *Préface de Francis Jammes*, Mercure de France, 1905.

La Retraite sentimentale, Mercure de France, 1907. *Retreat from Love*, Peter Owen, 1974, and Hamlyn Publ., 1984.

Les Vrilles de la vigne, Editions de la vie parisienne, 1908.

Colette

L'Ingénue libertine, Ollendorff, 1909 (made up of *Minne* and *Les Egarements de Minne*). Secker and Warburg, 1968; Penguin Books, 1972.

La Vagabonde, Ollendorff, 1911. *The Vagabond*, Secker and Warburg, 1954 and 1975; Penguin Books, 1972.

L'Envers du music-hall, Flammarion, 1913. *Music-Hall Sidelights*, with *My Apprenticeships*, Secker and Warburg, 1957; Penguin Books, 1967.

L'Entrave, Librarie des Lettres, 1913. *The Shackle*, Secker and Warburg, 1964; and Penguin Books, 1970; also Ballantine, 1982.

Prrou, Poucette et quelques autres, Librairie des Lettres, 1913.

La Paix chez les bêtes, Georges Crès et Cie., 1916. *Creatures Comfort* in *Creatures Great and Small* (new edn of the above).

Les Heures longues, A. Fayard, 1917.

Les Enfants dans les ruines, Editions de la Maison du Livre, 1917.

Dans la foule, Georges Crès et Cie, 1918.

Mitsou ou Comment l'esprit vient aux filles, A. Fayard, 1919. *Mitsou: or, The Education of Young Women; Music-Hall Sidelights*, Trans World, 1967. Also contains the play *En camarades*.

La Chambre éclairée, Edouard Joseph, 1920.

Chéri, A. Fayard, 1920. *Chéri* in *Chéri* and *The Last of Chéri*, Penguin Books, 1974; also Secker and Warburg, 1951 and 1969.

La Maison de Claudine, J. Ferenczi et fils, 1922. *My Mother's House* (and *Sido*) Penguin Books, 1966; also Secker and Warburg, 1953.

Le Voyage égoïste, Editions d'art Ed. Pelletan, 1922. *Journey For Myself; Selfish Memories*, Peter Owen, 1971.

Chéri, comédie en quatre actes, par Colette et Léopold Marchand, Librairie théâtrale, 1922.

La Vagabonde, comédie en quatre actes, par Colette et Léopold Marchand, Impr. de l'Illustration A. Chatenet, 1923.

Le Blé en herbe, Flammarion, 1923. *The Ripening Seed*, Secker and Warburg, 1955.

Rêverie du nouvel an, Stock, 1923.

La Femme cachée, Flammarion, 1924 (in *The Other Woman*, Peter Owen, 1971).

Aventures quotidiennes, Flammarion, 1924 (in *Journey For Myself*).

Quatre Saisons, Philippe Ortiz, 1925 (in *Journey For Myself*).

L'Enfant et les sortilèges, musique de Maurice Ravel, Durand et

Cie, 1925. *The Boy and the Magic,* adapted by Christopher Fry, Dennis Dobson, 1964.

La Fin de Chéri, Flammarion, 1926. *The Last of Chéri,* see above.

La Naissance du jour, Flammarion, 1928. *The Break of Day,* Secker and Warburg, 1961 and The Women's Press, 1979.

Renée Vivien, Abbeville, F. Paillart, 1928.

La Seconde, Ferenczi et Fils, 1929. *The Other One,* Penguin, 1972; also Secker and Warburg, 1960.

Sido, Editions Krâ, 1929 (*Sido,* in *My Mother's House*).

Histoires pour Bel-Gazou, Stock, 1930.

Douze dialogues de bêtes, Mercure de France, 1930 (*Creature Conversations* in *Creatures Great and Small*).

Paradis terrestres, Lausanne, Gonin et Cie, 1932.

La Treille muscate, Aimé Jourde, 1932.

Prisons et paradis, J. Ferenczi et fils, 1932 (Selections in *Places,* Peter Owen, 1970).

Ces Plaisirs, Ferenczi et fils, 1932; title changed to *Le Pur et l'impur,* 1941. *The Pure and the Impure,* Secker and Warburg, 1968.

La Chatte, Grasset, 1933. In *Gigi; The Cat,* Secker and Warburg, 1953; Penguin Books, 1958.

Duo, J. Ferenczi et fils, 1934. *Duo* in *Duo and The Toutonier,* The Women's Press, 1979; also Peter Owen, 1974.

La Jumelle noire, Ferenczi et fils, 1934–38.

Cahiers de Colette, Les Amis de Colette, 1935–36.

Discours de réception à l'Académie royale Belge de Langue et de Littérature française, Grasset, 1936.

Mes Apprentissages, Ferenczi et fils, 1936. *My Apprenticeships,* Secker and Warburg, 1957; Penguin Books, 1967.

Chats, Jacques Nam, 1936.

Splendeur des papillons, Plon, 1937.

Claudine et les contes de fée, Pour les Amis du Docteur Lucien Graux, 1937.

Bella-Vista, Ferenczi et fils, 1937. *Bella-Vista* in *The Stories of Colette,* tr. A. White, Secker and Warburg, 1958; also *Collected Stories,* tr. M. Ward etc., Secker and Warburg, 1984 and *Collected Stories,* ed. Robert Phelps, Penguin Books, 1985.

Le Toutounier, Ferenczi et fils, 1939. In *Duo and The Toutonier,* see above.

Chambre d'Hôtel, A. Fayard, 1940. *Chance Acquaintances* in *Julie de Carheilhan and Chance Acquaintances,* Secker and Warburg, 1953; Penguin Books, 1957.

Mes Cahiers, Aux Armes de France, 1941.

Journal à Rebours, A. Fayard, 1941. *Looking Backwards*, Peter Owen, 1975.

Julie de Carneilhan, A. Fayard, 1941. *Julie de Carneilhan*, in *Julie de Carneilhan and Chance Acquaintances*, see above.

De ma fenêtre, Aux Armes de France, 1942 (in *Looking Backwards*).

De la patte à l'aile, Editions Corrêa, 1943.

Flore et Pomone, Editions de la Galerie Charpentier, 1943.

Nudité, Bruxelles, Editions de la Mappemonde, 1943.

Le Képi, A. Fayard, 1943 (in *The Stories of Colette* or *Collected Stories*, as well as 'Le Tendron', *The Tender Shoot*, 'La Lune de pluie', *The Rainy Moon*, and others written in that period).

Broderie ancienne, Monaco, Editions du Rocher, 1944.

Gigi et autres nouvelles, Lausanne, La Guilde du Livre, 1944. *Gigi* in *Gigi; The Cat*, see above. (Stories, 'The Sick Child' and 'Photographer's Missus' in *The Stories of Colette* or *Collected Stories*).

Trois... Six... Neuf, Editions Corrêa, 1944 (Selections in *Places*, Peter Owen, 1970).

Belles Saisons, Editions de la Galerie Charpentier, 1945.

Une Amitié inattendue. Correspondance de Colette et de Francis Jammes, Editions Emile-Paul Frères, 1945.

L'Etoile Vesper, Geneva, Editions du Milieu du Monde, 1946. *The Evening Star*, Peter Owen, 1973.

Pour un herbier, Lausanne, Mermod, 1948. *For a Flower*, Weidenfeld and Nicolson, 1959.

Trait pour trait, Editions Le Fleuron, 1949.

Journal intermittent, Editions Le Fleuron, 1949 (Selections in *Places*, see above).

Le Fanal bleu, Ferenczi et fils, 1949. *The Blue Lantern*, Secker and Warburg, 1963. Extracts as well as from other autobiographical works of Colette in *Earthly Paradise*, ed. Robert Phelps, Secker and Warburg, 1966; Penguin Books, 1974.

La Fleur de l'âge, Editions Le Fleuron, 1949.

En Pays connu, Manuel Bruker, 1949 (Selections in *Places*, see above).

Chats de Colette, Albin Michel, 1949.

Gigi. Adapté pour la scène par Colette et Anita Loos, France-Illustration, 1954.

Posthumous works

Paysages et Portraits, Flammarion, 1958.

Selected Bibliography

Lettres à Hélène Picard, Flammarion, 1958
Lettres à Marguerite Moréno, Flammarion, 1959
Lettres de la Vagabonde, Flammarion, 1961
Lettres au petit corsaire, Flammarion, 1963
(Excerpts from all these in *Letters from Colette*, ed. Robert Phelps, Virago, 1982).
Contes des mille et un matins, Flammarion, 1970. *The Thousand and One Mornings*, Peter Owen, 1973.
Lettres à ses pairs, Flammarion, 1973 (Excerpts also in Virago, *Letters*...).
'Inédits en librairie', *Cahiers Colette No. 2*, Société des Amis de Colette, 1979.
Colette/Sido, *Lettres*, Editions des femmes, 1984.

Works on Colette and References

Colette bibliography is huge, and none is to date complete. I have only included works that I found directly useful, or of immediate interest. For an annotated bibliography to 1978, see Elaine Marks' section on Colette in *A Critical Bibliography of French Literature* (ed. Douglas W. Alden and Richard A. Brooks, Syracuse Un. Press, 1980, vol. 6, The twentieth century, Part 1: 679–716). For articles I found Paul d'Hollander's bibliography extremely useful, as well as that in the notes to Eisinger/McCarthy, 1981.

As for references, I have only included the works to which there is direct reference in the text. There is obviously a great deal else touching what I discuss, of which I am aware. But to be properly inclusive the bibliography would have had to be very large, and disproportionate to the size of this book.

As with the works of Colette, the place of publication is London or Paris unless otherwise stated.

Album Colette (to accompany the publication of vol. 1 of *Oeuvres*), Pléiade, Gallimard, 1984 (contains over 500 photographs).
Auffret, Séverine, *Des Couteaux contre des femmes. De l'excision*, Editions des femmes, 1983.
Auffret, Séverine, *Nous Clytemnestre*, Editions des femmes, 1985.
Beaumont, Germaine and André Parinaud, *Colette par elle-même*, Le Seuil, 'Ecrivains de toujours', 1951 (contains a moving

testimony by Germaine Beaumont, a friend of Colette).

Bernheimer, Charles and Claire Kahane (ed.), *In Dora's Case*, Virago, 1985.

Biolley-Godino, Marcelle, *L'Homme-objet chez Colette*, Klincksieck, 1972.

Blanchot, Maurice, *La Part du feu*, Gallimard, 1949.

Boncompain, Claude, *Colette*, Lyon, Confluences, 1945.

Bonmariage, Sylvain, *Willy, Colette et moi*, Frémanger, 1954 (Willy's ex-secretary and a witness hostile to Colette).

Caradec, François, *Feu Willy: avec et sans Colette*, J.J. Pauvert/Carrère, 1984.

Carco, Francis, *Colette 'mon ami'*, Rive Gauche, 1955.

Chalon, Jean, *Portrait d'une séductrice*, Stock, 1976.

Chauvière, Claude, *Colette*, F. Didot et Cie., 1931.

Cixous, Hélène, *La Jeune née* (in Cixous/Clément...), 10/18 1975.

Cixous, Hélène, 'The Laughter of the Medusa', in Marks and De Courtivron, 1981.

Cixous, Hélène, 'Castration or Decapitation', *Signs*, vol. 7, No. 1, 1981.

Cixous, Gagnon and Leclerc, *La Venue à l'écriture*, 10/18, 1977.

Clifford-Barney, Natalie, *Souvenirs indiscrets*, Flammarion, 1960.

Cocteau, Jean, *Colette, Discours de réception* à l'Académie royale de langue et de Littérature française de Belgique, Grasset, 1955.

Cottrell, Robert D., *Colette*, New York, Ungar, 1974 (a readable and intelligent study).

Crosland, Margaret, *Madame Colette, A Provincial in Paris*, Peter Owen, 1953.

Crosland, Margaret, *Colette: The Difficulty of Loving* (a fuller and further-reaching biography than the previous one), 1973.

Davidson, Cathy N. and E.M. Broner (eds.), *The Lost Tradition: Mothers and Daughters, in Literature*, New York, Ungar, 1980.

Davies, Margaret, *Colette*, Edinburgh and London, Oliver and Boyd, 1961.

Eisinger, Erica Mendelson and Mari Ward McCarthy (eds.), *Colette, The Woman, The Writer*, Un. Park and London, The Pennsylvania State University Press, 1981.

De Beauvoir, Simone, *The Second Sex*, trans. and ed. H.M. Parshley, Penguin Books, 1972.

De Beauvoir, Simone, *Mémoires d'une jeune fille rangée*, Gallimard, 1958.

Selected Bibliography

D'Hollander, Paul, *Colette: ses apprentissages*, Montréal, Presses universitaires de Montréal et Paris, Klincksieck, 1978.

Dormann, Geneviève, *Amoureuse Colette*, Herscher, 1984. Trans. as *Colette: A Passion For Life*, Thames & Hudson, 1985 (contains beautiful photographs).

Ellmann, Richard, *Ulysses on the Liffey*, Faber, 1972.

Engels, Friedrich, *The Origin of The Family, Private Property and the State*, Lawrence and Wishart, 1972 (first pub. 1884).

Federman, Lillian, *Surpassing the Love of Men: Romantic Friendship and Love between Women from the Renaissance to the Present*, The Women's Press, 1981.

Fillon, Amélie, *Colette*, La Caravelle, 1933.

Forestier, Louis, *Chemin vers 'La Maison de Claudine' et 'Sido'*, Société d'édition d'enseignement supérieur, 1968.

Fouque, Antoinette, 'Culture des femmes: Une gestation', *Des Femmes en mouvement Hebdo*, 53/54, Aug. 1981.

Fouque, Antoinette, 'Notre pays, notre terre de naissance, c'est le corps maternel, et c'est un corps de femme', *Des femmes en mouvement*, No. 1, May 1982 (10–14).

Freud, Sigmund, *The Interpretation of Dreams* (Vols. 4/5), 'Dora' (7), *Totem and Taboo* (13), *Beyond The Pleasure Principle* (18), 'Some Psychical Consequences of the Anatomical Distinction Between the Sexes', 1925 (19), *New Introductory Lectures on Psycho-Analysis* (22), 'Female Sexuality', 1931 (21), 'Splitting of the Ego in the Process of Defence', 1940 (23), all in *The Standard Edition*, The Hogarth Press, 1955–58.

Gilbert, Sandra and Susan Gubar, *The Madwoman in the Attic*, New Haven and London, Yale University Press, 1979.

Giry, Jacqueline, *Colette et l'art du discours intérieur*, La Pensée universelle, 1981.

Goudeket, Maurice, *La Douceur de vieillir*, Flammarion, 1965.

Goudeket, Maurice, *Près de Colette*, Flammarion, 1956.

Harris, Elaine, *L'Approfondissement de la sensualité dans l'oeuvre romanesque de Colette*, Nizet, 1973.

Hermann, Claudine, *Les Voleuses de langue*, Editions des femmes, 1976.

Houssa, Nicole, *Le Souci de l'expression chez Colette*, Bruxelles, Palais des Académies, 1958.

Houssa, Nicole, 'Balzac et Colette', *Revue d'Histoire littéraire de la France*, Jan.–Mar. 1960 (lists 23 titles from *La Comédie humaine* and references to 55 Balzacian characters in Colette).

Jouvenel, Bertrand de, *Un Voyageur dans le siècle*, Laffont, 1979.

Jung, C.G., *Man and His Symbols*, New York, Doubleday, 1979.

Jung, C.G., *Aspects of the Feminine*, Routledge and Kegan Paul, 1982.

Kappeler, Susanne, *The Pornography of Representation*, Oxford: Basil Blackwell/Polity Press, 1986.

Keller, Fernand and André Lautier, *Colette (Colette Willy). Son Oeuvre . . .*, Editions de la Nouvelle Revue critique, 1923.

Ketchum, Anne, *Colette ou la Naissance du jour. Etude d'un malentendu*, Minard, 1968.

Klein, Melanie *et al.*, *Developments in Psychoanalysis*, The Hogarth Press, 1952.

Kristéva, Julia, *La Révolution poétique du langage*, Le Seuil, 1977.

Kristéva, Julia, *Desire in Language: A Semiotic Approach to Literature and Art*, Oxford, Blackwell, 1980.

Lacan, Jacques, *Ecrits*, 2 vols., Le Point, 1966.

Lacan, Jacques, *Ecrits: A Selection*, Tavistock Publications, 1977.

Lacan, Jacques, *Séminaire Livre XI: Les Quatre concepts fondamentaux de la Psychanalyse*, Le Seuil, 1973. (In English at The Hogarth Press, 1977.)

Lacan, Jacques, *Séminaire Livre XX: Encore*, Le Seuil, 1975.

Larnac, Jean, *Colette, sa vie, son oeuvre*, Krâ, 1927.

Le Hardoin, Maria, *Colette*, Editions Universitaires, 1956.

Lejeune, Philippe, *Le Pacte autobiographique*, Le Seuil, 1975.

Lejeune, Philippe, *Je est un autre: l'autobiographie de la littérature aux médias*, Le Seuil, 1980.

Malinowski, Bronislaw, *The Ethnography of Malinowski: The Trobriand Islands 1915–1918*, Routledge and Kegan Paul, 1979.

Marks, Elaine, *Colette*, New Brunswick, Rutgers University, Press, 1960; London, Secker and Warburg, 1961 and Greenwood Press, 1982.

Marks, Elaine, 'Biography and Identification', MLA conference paper, delivered in Washington, 1984.

Marks, Elaine and Isabelle de Courtivron, *New French Feminisms*, Harvester Press, 1981.

Marx, Karl, *Capital*, 2 vols., Lawrence and Wishart, 1970.

Maulnier, Thierry, *Introduction à Colette*, La Palme, 1955.

Mitchell, Juliet, *Psychoanalysis and Feminism*, Pelican, 1975.

Mitchell, Yvonne, *Colette: A Taste for Life*, Weidenfeld and Nicolson, 1976 (contains some nice photographs). (Also New York, Harcourt Brace Jovanovich, 1975.)

Moers, Ellen, *Literary Women*, The Women's Press, 1978.

Selected Bibliography

Mugnier, Abbé, *Journal*, Mercure de France, 1985 (in *passim*, 394–559).

Oliver, Raymond, *Adieux, fourneaux*, Laffont, 1984; 242–58.

Parker, R. and G. Pollock, *Old Mistresses: Women, Art and Ideology*, Routledge and Kegan Paul, 1981.

Perche, Louis, *Colette*, Seghers, 1976.

Perry, Ruth, *Women, Letters and the Novel*, New York, AMS Press, 1980.

Raaphort-Rousseau, Madeleine, *Colette, sa vie et son art*, Nizet, 1964.

Reboux, Paul, *Colette ou le génie du style*, Rasmussen, 1925.

Resch, Yannick, *Corps féminin, corps textuel*, Klincksieck, 1973.

Rich, Adrienne, *On Lies, Secrets and Silence: Selected Prose 1966–1978*, Virago, 1980.

Richardson, Joanna, *Colette*, Methuen, 1983.

Sarde, Michèle, *Colette libre et entravée*, Stock, 1978. Trans. as *Colette: Free and Fettered*, New York, Morrow, 1980 and Michael Joseph, 1981. (The best documented and most complete of all biographies, also containing many critical insights, despite Angela Carter's caustic witty review in *Nothing Sacred*, Virago, 1982.)

Stambolian, G. and Elaine Marks (eds.), *Homosexualities in French Literature*, Cornell UP, 1979.

Stewart, Joan Hinde, *Colette*, Boston, Twayne Publishers, 1983 (compact, intelligent, one of the best monographs to date).

Sigl, Robert, *Colette...*, Editions des Belles lettres, 1924.

Tinter, Sylvie, *Colette et le Temps surmonté*, Genève, Slatkine, 1980.

Trahard, Pierre, *L'Art de Colette*, J. Renard, 1941.

Truc, Gonzague, *Madame Colette*, Corrêa, 1941.

Veschambre, Christiane, 'Affections de la langue-mère', *Land* 5/6, 1983.

Van Casselaer, Catherine, *Lot's Wife, Lesbian Paris, 1890–1914*, Liverpool: The Janus Press, 1986.

Virmaux, Alain and Odette, *Colette au cinéma*, Flammarion, 1975. Trans. as *Colette At The Movies: Criticism and Screenplays*, New York, Ungar, 1985.

Viel, Marie-Jeanne, *Colette au temps des Claudine, récit*, Les Publications essentielles, 1978.

Ward Jouve, Nicole, *'The Streetcleaner': The Yorkshire Ripper Case On Trial*, Marion Boyars, 1986 (for a study of the links between masculinity and death, and of the destructive way in which the semiotic and the symbolic may combine).

Colette

Willy, *Indiscrétions et commentaires sur les 'Claudine'*, Pro Amicis, 1962.

Recent albums/Reviews on Colette

Bulletins de la Société des amis de Colette en Puisaye, 1–12, Saint-Sauveur-en-Puisaye, 1966–72.

Cahiers Colette esp. 3/4, 'Colloque de Dijon 1979', Flammarion, 1981.

Masques, album spécial, 1984.

Colette en tournée (postcards from Colette to Sido, 1905–12), Editions Persona, 1984.

Index

Index